P9-DEI-630

NEW DIRECTIONS FOR PROGRAM EVALUATION
A Publication of the American Evaluation Association

Nick L. Smith, *Syracuse University*
EDITOR-IN-CHIEF

Varieties of Investigative Evaluation

Nick L. Smith
Syracuse University

EDITOR

Number 56, Winter 1992

JOSSEY-BASS PUBLISHERS
San Francisco

VARIETIES OF INVESTIGATIVE EVALUATION
Nick L. Smith (ed.)
New Directions for Program Evaluation, no. 56
Nick L. Smith, Editor-in-Chief

Microfilm copies of issues and articles are available in 16mm and 35mm, as well as microfiche in 105mm, through University Microfilms Inc., 300 North Zeeb Road, Ann Arbor, Michigan 48106.

LC 85-644749   ISSN 0164-7989   ISBN 1-55542-741-3

NEW DIRECTIONS FOR PROGRAM EVALUATION is part of The Jossey-Bass Education Series and is published quarterly by Jossey-Bass Inc., Publishers (publication number USPS 449-050).

EDITORIAL CORRESPONDENCE should be sent to the editor-in-chief, William R. Shadish, Department of Psychology, Memphis State University, Memphis, Tennessee 38152.

 The paper used in this journal is acid-free and meets the strictest guidelines in the United States for recycled paper (50 percent recycled waste, including 10 percent post-consumer waste). Manufactured in the United States of America.

INSTRUCTIONS TO CONTRIBUTORS

NEW DIRECTIONS FOR PROGRAM EVALUATION (NDPE), a quarterly sourcebook, is an official publication of the American Evaluation Association. As such, NDPE publishes empirical, methodological, and theoretical work on all aspects of program evaluation and related fields. Substantive areas may include any area of social programming such as mental health, education, job training, medicine, or public health, but may also extend the boundaries of evaluation to such topics as product evaluation, personnel evaluation, policy analysis, or technology assessment. In all cases, the focus on evaluation is more important than the particular substantive topic.

NDPE does not consider or publish unsolicited single manuscripts. Each issue of NDPE is devoted to a single topic, with contributions solicited, organized, reviewed, and edited by a guest editor. Issues may take any of several forms, such as a series of related chapters, a monograph, or a long article followed by brief critical commentaries. In all cases, proposals must follow a specific format, which can be obtained from the editor-in-chief. These proposals are sent to members of the editorial board, and to relevant substantive experts, for peer review. This process may result in rejection, acceptance, or a recommendation to revise and resubmit. However, NDPE is committed to working constructively with potential guest editors to help them develop acceptable proposals. Close contact with the editor-in-chief is encouraged during proposal preparation and generation.

COPIES OF NDPE's "Guide for Proposal Development" and "Proposal Format" can be obtained from the editor-in-chief:

William R. Shadish, Editor-in-Chief
New Directions for Program Evaluation
Department of Psychology
Memphis State University
Memphis, TN 38152
Office: 901-678-4687
FAX: 901-678-2579
Bitnet: SHADISHWR@MEMSTVX1

CONTENTS

EDITOR'S NOTES

In many sectors, the practice of evaluation—whether qualitative or quantitative, postpositivist or phenomenological, experimental or field-based—increasingly has become investigative in order to study dynamic phenomena, serve shifting client needs, and allow greater flexibility in response to changing contextual influences. As a result of the pragmatic difficulties of evaluation practice, idealized images of confirmatory studies of stable interventions have been replaced by patterns of investigative studies of changing programs and fluctuating information needs.

Although evaluation has always been investigative in important ways, the purpose of this volume, *Varieties of Investigative Evaluation,* is to highlight evaluations that are especially investigative in nature in order to examine how common elements of these studies can be used to improve evaluation theory and practice. Our intent is not to coin new terms or to attempt to create a new form of evaluation but rather to reflect on changes in existing practice and to highlight investigative elements that have been underemphasized in evaluations to date. Since our insights about the investigative nature of evaluation have arisen mostly from reflections on practice, we employ a compatible format in this volume.

In Chapter One, I present a brief historical review of the emergence of investigative approaches to evaluation. I then identify various aspects of investigative inquiry that can be seen in the examples of the other chapters in this volume. For example, I describe investigative inquiry as a recursively emergent, problem-focused process that is alternately exploratory and confirmatory, leading to the development of multiple lines of argument to explain or solve the problem addressed.

In the next five chapters, the authors report on investigative evaluations that use a range of methods in different contexts at the local, regional, national, and international levels. The iterative, problem-solving nature of investigative evaluation is seen in the four case examples provided by David M. Fetterman in Chapter Two. Fetterman's examples explore the relationships among evaluation, investigative inquiry, and litigation. He provides intriguing illustrations of the evaluator in a local private investigator role.

In Chapter Three, Thomas A. Schwandt portrays the investigative evaluator in both consultant and field researcher roles. He contrasts the use of evaluation audits and case studies as alternative approaches to framing investigative evaluations.

In Chapter Four, Michael F. Mangano describes investigative evaluation at the national level. He illustrates the investigative dimensions of the complementary roles of criminal investigators and program evaluators in improving federal health care services.

In Chapter Five, Debra J. Rog also examines the use of investigative procedures at the national level. Her focus is more on the use of investigative procedures in the formation of federal policy and the development of national programs than on the assessment of service delivery.

The venue changes to the international scene in Chapter Six. Here, David W. Chapman discusses the necessity of investigative procedures when evaluating international technical assistance projects.

Finally, in Chapter Seven, Deborah M. Fournier provides an analysis of the investigative elements of the preceding chapters, comparing and contrasting the varieties of investigative strategies presented in this volume.

Together, the chapters provide diverse images of the investigative evaluator as detective (Fetterman), ethnographer and management consultant (Schwandt), national program monitor (Mangano), national policy analyst (Rog), and international development specialist (Chapman). Although contexts, purposes, and methods vary across these examples, they all share elements of investigative inquiry. Collectively, they illustrate current varieties of investigative evaluation.

Nick L. Smith
Editor

NICK L. SMITH *is professor in the School of Education at Syracuse University and past editor-in-chief of* New Directions for Program Evaluation.

A description of the characteristics of investigative inquiry can illuminate examples of evaluation practice that are increasingly investigative.

Aspects of Investigative Inquiry in Evaluation

Nick L. Smith

> Investigate: to examine the particulars of in an attempt to learn the facts about something hidden, unique, or complex, especially in search of a motive, cause, or culprit.
> —*Random House Dictionary of the English Language,* 1967, p. 749

> Investigate: fr L *investigare* to track, fr *in* + *vestigium* foot print, track.
> —*Webster's New Collegiate Dictionary,* 1975, p. 608

The above definitions suggest that in using investigative inquiry in evaluation, evaluators are likely to follow tracks or indicators in pursuit of information about something complex and hidden from view. "To investigate" is to search into, to inspect, to explore, in contrast with to test, to confirm. Investigative evaluations are thus more likely to be undertaken for exploratory than for confirmatory purposes.

Further, the objects of investigative evaluations are likely to be complex, unique, and hidden from view because they are dynamic, historical, or simply largely unknown. Thus, direct measurement is not likely to be feasible, and confirmatory tests are probably premature. The lack of direct accessibility is likely to require greater reliance on inferential methods, intuitive insight, and expertise than on the explicit procedural guidelines of deductive approaches.

While all evaluations can be considered investigative in some sense, the focus in this chapter is on evaluations that are distinctively investigative in nature. The purpose here is to provide a brief overview of the emerging investigative theme in evaluation theory, practice, and methods and to highlight the characteristics that make some evaluations more investigative than others. The evaluations reported elsewhere in this volume reflect these investigative characteristics in varying degrees and thereby provide the opportunity for studying the nature and variations of investigative aspects of evaluation practice.

The Investigative Theme in Evaluation

Over the past thirty years, both quantitative and qualitative forms of evaluation methodology have become increasingly investigative. Cook and Shadish (1986), for example, trace this trend from the late 1960s through the mid-1980s. Over this period, the need for methodological diversity in evaluation has become increasingly recognized and accepted. Shadish, Cook, and Leviton (1991, p. 469) summarize the reasons for this shift, concluding that regardless of whether quantitative, qualitative, or mixed method procedures are employed, "multiple tentative probes are the watchword, replacing conceptions based on theory-free observation, single definitive tests, and crucial single studies."

In the early 1960s, the randomized experiment was generally considered the only proper method for the evaluation of causal claims (see Rossi and Wright, 1977). In response to severe criticism of the experimental approach on pragmatic, methodological, and ethical grounds (see, for example, Smith, 1981, for a summary of criticisms and responses), evaluators turned to the development of stronger quasi-experimental designs as an alternative. Subsequent criticism of quasi experimentation led to greater attention to methods of causal modeling—first to the simple fitting of models and then to the development of multiple, competing models incorporating multiple measures of constructs. Quantitative analysis has become markedly more investigative with the introduction and popularity of Tukey's (1977) exploratory data analysis procedures.

Evaluations in general became more investigative with the rise of qualitative approaches to evaluation and their general focus on noncausal questions. Evaluations also became more service-oriented than inquiry-oriented. Client and stakeholder-centered approaches were developed (for example, Stake, 1975; Guba and Lincoln, 1981; Patton, 1986), drawing on qualitative methodologies from postpositivist (Yin, 1984), ethnographic (Fetterman, 1984), and phenomenological (Bogdan and Biklen, 1982) traditions. Qualitative evaluations have also become increasingly investigative, with advocacy for multiple-case studies and multiple observers, attempts to reconcile differences in perspectives, and the conduct of openly investigative qualitative meta-evaluations (for example, Stake, 1986).

The recognition that important evaluation questions often change during the conduct of a study has led theorists to argue for procedures that are less preordinant and fixed and more flexible. For example, Smith (1990) has identified several types of flexibility possible in creating adaptive evaluation designs. Even traditionally quantitative theorists have argued for approaches capable of addressing questions that evolve over time and that enable one to answer many different types of questions within a single study. For example, Cronbach (1982) favors flexible evaluation designs and urges us to consider the methods of journalists and historians (see Shadish, Cook, and Leviton, 1991, for a discussion of Cronbach's position). Also, evaluation writers have begun advocating the use of multiple strategies in evaluation, including multiple studies (Cronbach and others, 1980), a multimodel (Scriven, 1983), patched-up designs (Cordray, 1986), postpositivist critical multiplism (Cook, 1985; Shadish, Cook, and Houts, 1986), and other multimethod variations (Mark and Shotland, 1987). Shadish, Cook, and Leviton (1991) argue that the most integrated resolutions of the problem of selection from multiple evaluation alternatives are seen in the work of Rossi (see Rossi and Freeman, 1989) and Cronbach (1982), who have developed contingency theories of evaluation that specify the conditions under which the different evaluation practices are effective (see Smith, in press).

Techniques for conducting the more investigative elements of evaluations have emerged as part of the greater diversification of evaluation methodology in quantitative (Cordray, 1986), qualitative (Guba and Lincoln, 1989), and ethnographic (Fetterman, 1989) domains. Other methodological work has included attempts to adapt methods from such areas as investigative journalism (Levine, 1980; Guba, 1981; Smith, 1982b) for use in evaluation, to assess the suitability of various evaluation models in investigative settings (Smith and Hauer, 1990), and to develop an explicit logic of investigative inquiry in evaluation (Scriven, 1974).

Whether quantitative or qualitative, postpositivist or phenomenological, or experimental or field-based, evaluation methods have become increasingly investigative. This is a result, in part, of thoughtful reflection on the effectiveness of evaluation practice and on the limits of our knowledge about the development, operation, and evaluation of social and educational programs. Prior methods have proved helpful but insufficient in the task of handling the range of evaluation questions, problems, and contexts confronted by the practitioner. The recognition of methodological limitations has led to a greater appreciation for the role of discovery in evaluation and to a general movement away from preordinant, goal-centered, highly controlled approaches and toward strategies requiring greater flexibility of design, whereby studies are conducted in situ and adapted in process in response to accumulating knowledge about the program and the stakeholders' interests: "The generalization of this point is to the use of 'emergent,' 'cascading,' or 'rolling' designs, where the whole design is varied enroute as appropriate. . . . Note that the traditional response to what are here called 'investigatory' designs is to call them 'exploratory' with the implication that they will eventually lead to serious formulation and testing of a hypothesis—the 'real' research. They *are* real research" (Scriven, 1991, pp. 154–155).

Characteristics of Investigative Inquiry

In this section, I identify several characteristic aspects of investigative inquiry. Although there is much that could be said about each characteristic, space restrictions preclude a lengthy discussion. The characteristics are only introduced here as a possible framework for illuminating examples of investigative evaluation, such as those presented in Chapters Two through Six in this volume. Although the characteristics identified here are conceptually distinct, in the practice of investigative inquiry they are inextricably interconnected.

Investigative Contexts. Any inquiry takes place within a number of contexts, including not only the local context of the particular study but also the broader social, historical contexts within which the study and other studies of a similar type are conducted. To fully understand the meaning and method of a given investigative study, we must recognize the significant elements of the local setting as well as appreciate the broader social role that the particular type of investigative inquiry plays in society (see Smith, 1982a, 1991).

Investigative Purposes. Investigative inquiry is, of course, a purposeful activity, that is, a series of actions designed to achieve some intent, outcome, or goal. Scriven (1967) distinguishes between the goal of evaluation (which is to assess worth) and the possible roles of evaluation (for example, accountability and program improvement). A similar distinction can be made here between the goal of investigative inquiry (which is to gain knowledge about something hidden) and the many roles played by investigative inquiry (for example, in investigative journalism, forensic medicine, applied social research, and program evaluation). Each role played by investigative inquiry comprises a complex set of concepts, rules of practice, and criteria for assessing the quality of an investigation. The nature of an investigative study is different when conducted as part of investigative journalism than when conducted as part of investigative social science. The roles are different, although the investigative goal is the same; metaphorically, one might say that a different investigative "game" is being played in each instance. Thus, to understand fully the purpose of a given investigative study, we must understand both its local goal and its broader role or game. Note the interconnectedness of an investigative study's purpose and its contexts of application.

Investigative Process. In many instances, the process of conducting an investigative study best distinguishes this type of study from other forms of inquiry. Investigative inquiry tends to be more *problem-oriented* than question-focused. Although many questions may arise during the course of the inquiry, the investigation is, on the whole, not driven by questions but rather by the problem to be solved, such as finding a lost child, isolating the cause of a disease, or discovering which summer program activities are contributing most to the retention of college freshmen. Investigative studies tend to be more holistic than reductionistic in the sense that although they are often extremely detailed, the details are used to build a unified understanding of the problem under study. Hence, cases or stories are frequently used as recording and communication devices. Narrative is an effective means of conveying the integrated details of context, participants, conditions, events, actions, motives, and consequences in an overall recounting of a specific case.

An investigative study reflects an *emergent design.* Although there may be likely strategies or heuristics for uncovering hidden elements, one cannot determine a priori which investigative techniques will be effective. Prior specification of procedural details is not possible. Investigative designs are thus often iterative, cyclical, and sequential, although not sequential in a strictly linear sense. Investigative designs might be described as *recursively* sequential, that is, what to do next is determined on the basis of the results of what is currently done.[1] Thus, a study may take an unexpected turn, unforeseen questions may arise, and different methods may be selected as a result of what is learned as the investigation proceeds. For example, in an evaluation of emergency telephone hot line services for runaway youth, an incidental call to a hot line evidenced such great difficulty in actually getting through to the hot line personnel that the evaluators initiated a study of hot line access, an issue that was not previously known to be problematic (U.S. Department of Health and Human Services, 1983). Smith and Hauer (1990) have discussed the extent to which some evaluation models are more responsive to emergent information about the evaluand (for example, Scriven's, 1973, goal-free model), while other models are more responsive to emergent information about stakeholder needs (for example, Stake's, 1975, responsive model).

Investigative designs are generally thought of as primarily exploratory, which they are in a broad sense, but the actual investigative process is *alternately exploratory and confirmatory.*[2] Questions are identified and answered, leading to still further questions. Hunches, leads, or hypotheses arise and are then pursued, tested, or disconfirmed, raising new possibilities to consider. The investigative process often proceeds, first, with a broadening or expanding of the field of inquiry until the outer boundaries of the investigation are established, followed by a consideration of multiple alternatives, with a gradual narrowing of the inquiry as alternatives are discarded. This process involves the development of working theories or explanations, the construction of alternative hypotheses, and the testing and refining of both theories and hypotheses. This work may proceed on both formal explicit and informal tacit levels. It is alternately discovery-oriented and invention-oriented, exploratory and confirmatory.

Another characteristic of the process of investigative inquiry is the development of one or more *lines of argument*. These lines of argument are constructed and tested over time as knowledge and understanding accumulate, and they result from the recursively emergent, exploratory and confirmatory process just described. The best supported lines of argument at the termination of the investigation come to serve as explanations or solutions to the problem on which the investigation was focused. The claims within these lines of argument are often justified more on the basis of informal than on formal logic (see, for example, Fournier and Smith's [1992] application of Toulmin's [1958] informal logic procedures to the justification of claims arising under different evaluation approaches). The entire investigative process is directed toward production of warranted claims and convincing lines of argument that explain or solve the particular problem under investigation.[3]

Investigative Means. In order to carry out this investigative process, one needs both mental powers or abilities and procedural or methodological tools. The methodological tools needed depend, in part, on the investigative game or role that the evaluator is playing (for example, investigative journalist or forensic pathologist) and on the nature of the phenomenon under investigation (for example, a geological investigation of continental drift, an interpretation of the figures on the Portland Vase found in 1697, or an explanation of the influences precipitating the current reformation of Eastern Europe). Although the methodological tools of investigative inquiry are incredibly diverse across these areas of application, the necessary mental powers are surprisingly similar and can be described under four general categories.

First, an essential aspect of any investigative activity is the prior and ongoing accumulation of *knowledge*. Knowledge about the phenomenon under study is, of course, a prerequisite to, the purpose for, and the end result of the investigation. But knowledge of both the local context of the phenomenon and the broader social, historical context of the investigation is also needed. Further, knowledge of the game or role played by each particular form of investigation is necessary for successful participation. For example, in order to investigate an incident of alleged child abuse, one must acquire knowledge about the specific case (allegations, circumstances, events, evidence, and so on) as well as have knowledge of the local context of the case (for example, the involvement of an influential community leader) and of broader social values, psychological understandings, and legal precedents in current society. The nature of a "proper" investigation (that is, playing a particular investigative game well) depends on whether one is investigating the incident as a lawyer to protect the child's safety and rights, as a journalist to inform the public of a significant story, or as a social worker to design a therapeutic intervention for the child and family. Each form of investigation requires different types of knowledge—both public and personal knowledge and both propositional and tacit knowledge from study and experience. Methodological tools of investigative inquiry (observations, interviews, tracking, and so on) can provide only certain types of the needed information.

Second, the mental powers needed to conduct investigative inquiry include the powers of *observation*. I do not mean observation in the narrow sense of data collection but rather in the more profound sense of knowledge about what to look for, the ability to recognize the meaning and significance of what is seen, the ability to perceive and interpret. Obviously, these powers of observation presuppose much prior knowledge and experience. Methodological tools can supplement but never supplant the mental powers of observation.

Third, the powers of *reasoning* are needed for any investigative inquiry, especially when the intent of that inquiry is to build a line of argument or chain of reasoning that fully explains a problem within the confines of a particular context and inquiry game. Characteristic of investigative inquiry is the simultaneous development and testing of multiple lines of argument. There has been extensive historical treatment in science and philosophy of methods for developing warranted claims within multiple lines of practical inference (for example, Chamberlin, 1897; Toulmin, 1958; Platt, 1964), including recent discussions applicable to the use of investigative procedures in evaluation (for example, Scriven, 1974, 1986; Sebeok and Umiker-Sebeok, 1983). Although a discussion of this extensive literature is beyond the scope of this chapter, it is important to note the relevance of this work to the ever-present concern with the justification of claims within the increasingly diverse methods of evaluation. This historical work holds special promise for clarifying the nature of claims made in investigative evaluations.

Fourth, the powers of *intuition* are perhaps the category of mental abilities least often acknowledged in discussions of methodology but most often highlighted in anecdotes of investigative insight. The important role of intuition and even the conditions of its occurrence in scientific investigation have been long recognized (see Beveridge, 1957); intuition serves as an especially powerful aid in investigative studies because of the frequent lack of direct access to the phenomena of interest.

These four mental abilities or powers—knowledge, observation, reasoning, and intuition—are employed in the alternately exploratory and confirmatory, recursively emergent process of investigative inquiry to develop and justify claims in the construction of multiple lines of argument designed to fully explain a problem that has been posed within the given context of a particular investigative game. The methodological tools and techniques employed in inquiry are developed as a result of these abilities, and they, in turn, reciprocally empower these abilities, just as my hands create a hammer, which in turn increases the power of my hands. The choice of methodological tools in an investigation depends on the given context, rules of the particular investigative game, and the nature of the phenomenon of interest, but the underlying mental powers of inquiry (knowledge, observation, reasoning, and intuition) remain the same. Full acquisition of methodological tools identifies one as a master technician; full development of one's mental powers identifies one as a substantive expert.

All formal inquiry requires the development of expertise. Powerful methods (techniques) do not replace expertise (developed mental powers), even though the methods may be more visible to the naive observer. Investigative inquiry often involves phenomena that are less known, more hidden, intractable, and methodologically less accessible. When methodological tools and procedural guidelines are insufficient or unavailable, our reliance on mental powers, on our expertise rather than on our methods, is more evident.

Conclusion

Most major approaches to evaluation appear to have become increasingly investigative in recent years. The preceding discussion has provided a framework for examining the aspects of investigative inquiry appearing in evaluation work: (1) Investigative contexts: Both local and broad social, historical contexts are relevant. (2) Investigative purposes: The goal is to uncover something hidden, through the various roles or inquiry games played by investigators (journalists, pathologists, social scientists, and so on). (3) Investigative process: The process is problem-oriented, recursively emergent, alternatively exploratory and confirmatory, and focused on the development of lines of argument. (4) Investigative means: The methods or techniques used depend on the investigative context, the game being played, the phenomena of interest, but all investigations require the mental powers of knowledge, observation, reasoning, and intuition.

The following five chapters contain multiple examples of investigative evaluations that reflect these aspects in varying degrees. The reader is encouraged to use this framework to illuminate the investigative aspects of those examples. The concluding chapter in this volume provides a formal analysis of these examples using selected investigative aspects from the present chapter.

Notes

1. The phrase recursively sequential or emergent refers to a process analogous to a recursion formula in mathematics in which one determines the next term in a sequence from one or more preceding terms, or to a recursive definition in logic in which the repeated application of a set of rules results in the meaning of the definiendum being uniquely determined in terms of ideas already familiar.

2. To the extent that the term *design* refers to a preset procedural guide, investigative studies may not be said to have designs except in a loose sense, and then only as known retrospectively (Smith, 1990).

3. While the primary purpose of an investigative study is typically the complete explanation of a given case, the relevance of findings to other cases can be argued on the basis of naturalistic generalization (see Stake and Trumbull, 1982) or on the basis of similarities of the particulars of the given case to a class of similar cases. Variations of this argument include Brunswik's notion of ecological validity (1956) and Cronbach's (1982) discussion of extrapolation of findings through the study of subpopulations (see also Smith and Caulley, 1979). The primary basis for the generalization of findings from investigative studies, however, is probably through appeals to causal explanations. Explanations of the processes by which a particular effect or outcome was produced enable one to consider other circumstances where similar processes may be operational. For example, Shadish, Cook, and Leviton (1991, especially pp. 347–348) discuss Cronbach's use of both qualitative and quantitative methods for achieving extrapolation of results based on such explanations.

References

Beveridge, W.I.B. *The Art of Scientific Investigation.* New York: Vintage, 1957.

Bogdan, R. C., and Biklen, S. K. *Qualitative Research for Education.* Needham Heights, Mass.: Allyn & Bacon, 1982.

Brunswik, E. *Representative Design of Psychological Experiments.* (2nd ed.) Berkeley: University of California Press, 1956.

Chamberlin, T. C. "The Method of Multiple Working Hypotheses." *Journal of Geology,* 1897, 5, 837–848.

Cook, T. D. "Post-Positivist Critical Multiplism." In L. Shotland and M. Mark (eds.), *Social Science and Social Policy.* Newbury Park, Calif.: Sage, 1985.

Cook, T. D., and Shadish, W. R. "Program Evaluation: The Worldly Science." *Annual Review of Psychology,* 1986, 37, 193–232.

Cordray, D. S. "Quasi-Experimental Analysis: A Mixture of Methods and Judgment." In W.M.K. Trochim (ed.), *Advances in Quasi-Experimental Design and Analysis.* New Directions for Program Evaluation, no. 31. San Francisco: Jossey-Bass, 1986.

Cronbach, L. J. *Designing Evaluations of Educational and Social Programs.* San Francisco: Jossey-Bass, 1982.

Cronbach, L. J., Ambron, S. R., Dornbusch, S. M., Hess, R. D., Hornik, R. C., Phillips, D. C., Walker, D. F., and Weiner, S. S. *Toward Reform of Program Evaluation: Aims, Methods, and Institutional Arrangements.* San Francisco: Jossey-Bass, 1980.

Fetterman, D. M. (ed.). *Ethnography in Educational Evaluation.* Newbury Park, Calif.: Sage, 1984.

Fetterman, D. M. *Ethnography: Step by Step.* Newbury Park, Calif.: Sage, 1989.

Fournier, D. M., and Smith, N. L. "Clarifying the Merits of Argument in Evaluation Practice." Paper presented at the annual meeting of the American Educational Research Association, San Francisco, Apr. 1992.

Guba, E. G. "Investigative Journalism." In N. L. Smith (ed.), *New Techniques for Evaluation*. Newbury Park, Calif.: Sage, 1981.

Guba, E. G., and Lincoln, Y. S. *Effective Evaluation: Improving the Usefulness of Evaluation Results Through Responsive and Naturalistic Approaches*. San Francisco: Jossey-Bass, 1981.

Guba, E. G., and Lincoln, Y. S. *Fourth Generation Evaluation*. Newbury Park, Calif.: Sage, 1989.

Levine, M. "Investigative Reporting as a Research Method: An Analysis of Bernstein and Woodward's *All the President's Men*." *American Psychologist*, 1980, *35* (7), 626–638.

Mark, M. M., and Shotland, R. L. (eds.). *Multiple Methods in Program Evaluation*. New Directions for Program Evaluation, no. 35. San Francisco: Jossey-Bass, 1987.

Patton, M. Q. *Utilization-Focused Evaluation*. (2nd ed.) Newbury Park, Calif.: Sage, 1986.

Platt, J. R. "Strong Inference." *Science*, 1964, *146* (3642), 347–353.

Random House Dictionary of the English Language. (Unabridged ed.) New York: Random House, 1967.

Rossi, R. H., and Freeman, H. E. *Evaluation: A Systematic Approach*. (4th ed.) Newbury Park, Calif.: Sage, 1989.

Rossi, R. H., and Wright, S. R. "Evaluation Research: An Evaluation of Theory, Practice, and Politics." *Evaluation Quarterly*, 1977, *1* (1), 5–52.

Scriven, M. S. "The Methodology of Evaluation." In R. W. Tyler, R. M. Gagne, and M. S. Scriven (eds.), *Perspectives of Curriculum Evaluation*. Skokie, Ill.: Rand McNally, 1967.

Scriven, M. S. "Goal-Free Evaluation." In E. R. House (ed.), *School Evaluation: The Politics and Process*. Berkeley, Calif.: McCutchan, 1973.

Scriven, M. S. "Evaluation Perspectives and Procedures." In W. J. Popham (ed.), *Evaluation in Education: Current Applications*. Berkeley, Calif.: McCutchan, 1974.

Scriven, M. S. "Evaluation Ideologies." In G. F. Madaus, M. S. Scriven, and D. L. Stufflebeam (eds.), *Evaluation Models*. Boston: Kluwer-Nijhoff, 1983.

Scriven, M. S. "Probative Logic." In F. H. van Eemeren, R. Grootendorst, J. A. Blair, and C. A. Willard (eds.), *Argumentation: Across the Lines of Discipline*. Proceedings of the Conference on Argumentation. Dordrecht, The Netherlands: Foris, 1986.

Scriven, M. S. *Evaluation Thesaurus*. (4th ed.) Newbury Park, Calif.: Sage, 1991.

Sebeok, T. A., and Umiker-Sebeok, J. " 'You Know My Method': A Juxtaposition of Charles S. Peirce and Sherlock Holmes." In U. Eco and T. A. Sebeok (eds.), *The Sign of the Three: Dupin, Holmes, Peirce*. Bloomington: Indiana University Press, 1983.

Shadish, W. R., Cook, T. D., and Houts, A. C. "Quasi-Experimentation in a Critical Multiplist Mode." In W.M.K. Trochim (ed.), *Advances in Quasi-Experimental Design and Analysis*. New Directions for Program Evaluation, no. 31. San Francisco: Jossey-Bass, 1986.

Shadish, W. R., Cook, T. D., and Leviton, L. C. *Foundations of Program Evaluation*. Newbury Park, Calif.: Sage, 1991.

Smith, N. L. "The Feasibility and Desirability of Experimental Methods in Evaluation." *Evaluation and Program Planning*, 1981, *3* (4), 251–256.

Smith, N. L. "The Context of Evaluation Practice in State Departments of Education." *Educational Evaluation and Policy Analysis*, 1982a, *4* (3), 373–386.

Smith, N. L. "Investigative Tracking in Library Evaluation." In N. L. Smith (ed.), *Field Assessments of Innovative Evaluation Methods*. New Directions for Program Evaluation, no. 13. San Francisco: Jossey-Bass, 1982b.

Smith, N. L. "Flexibility in the Evaluation of Emergent Programs." *Studies in Educational Evaluation*, 1990, *16*, 209–229.

Smith, N. L. "The Context of Investigations in Cross-Cultural Evaluation." *Studies in Educational Evaluation*, 1991, *17*, 3–21.

Smith, N. L. "Evaluation Models and Approaches." In T. Husen and T. N. Postlethwaite (eds.), *The International Encyclopedia of Education.* (2nd ed.) Oxford, England: Pergamon Press, in press.

Smith, N. L., and Caulley, D. N. "Post-Evaluation Determination of a Program's Generalizability." *Evaluation and Program Planning,* 1979, 2 (4), 297–302.

Smith, N. L., and Hauer, D. M. "The Applicability of Selected Evaluation Models to Evolving, Investigative Designs." *Studies in Educational Evaluation,* 1990, *16,* 489–500.

Stake, R. E. (ed.). *Evaluating the Arts in Education: A Responsive Approach.* Columbus, Ohio: Merrill, 1975.

Stake, R. E. *Quieting Reform.* Urbana: University of Illinois Press, 1986.

Stake, R. E., and Trumbull, D. J. "Naturalistic Generalizations." *Review Journal of Philosophy and Social Science,* 1982, 7, 1–12.

Toulmin, S. E. *The Uses of Argument.* Cambridge, England: Cambridge University Press, 1958.

Tukey, J. W. *Exploratory Data Analysis.* Reading, Mass.: Addison-Wesley, 1977.

U.S. Department of Health and Human Services. Office of Inspector General. *Runaway and Homeless Youth.* Washington, D.C.: Government Printing Office, 1983.

Webster's New Collegiate Dictionary. Springfield, Mass.: Merriam-Webster, 1975.

Yin, R. K. *Case Study Research: Design and Methods.* Newbury Park, Calif.: Sage, 1984.

NICK L. SMITH *is professor in the School of Education at Syracuse University and past editor-in-chief of* New Directions for Program Evaluation.

Investigative evaluation can untangle a web of misdirection and intrigue and weave a strong fabric of evidence.

Investigative Evaluation and Litigation

David M. Fetterman

In making judgments about such sacred cultural categories as money, reputation, and even physical safety, evaluators often make objective, if unflattering, remarks about sensitive issues. Although clarity and precision in phrasing can minimize the client's defensiveness—as well as enhance an evaluator's effectiveness (Fetterman, 1989a)—arguments that have no easy resolution sometimes arise. In a litigious environment, disagreements between sponsor and evaluator about how to conduct an evaluation, for example, may require legal intervention. Similarly, evaluation findings documenting fraud or other improprieties may propel a study into the courtroom.

This discussion presents four case examples in which evaluation led to or was conducted in anticipation of legal maneuvers and litigation. The examples mark different stages of the evaluation-litigation life cycle. In the first example, a dispute between the evaluator and the sponsor was focused on methodological issues. This case highlights legal intervention before the evaluation is even off the ground. The second example involves fraud, and the evaluator (in the role of an auditor) conducted the entire investigation in anticipation of litigation. This example highlights investigative concepts such as immersion as well as the usefulness in many instances of simple common sense. It also emphasizes the role of archival material and of an audit trail. The third example, like the second, concerns fraud and involves conflicts between the evaluator (again in the role of an auditor) and a suspect under investigation. The case illustrates legal intervention during the actual investigation. The final example demonstrates how a complainant's dissatisfaction with evaluation findings can result in a

New Directions for Program Evaluation, no. 56, Winter 1992 © Jossey-Bass Publishers

lawsuit after the study is completed. One of the common threads running through all of these studies is the evaluator's absolute reliance on investigative techniques and approaches to untangle a web of misdirection and intrigue and to weave a strong fabric of evidence.

Dispute with the Sponsor

Despite tough competition, including that from the Educational Testing Service, the sponsor accepted the proposal of my firm to conduct an ethnographic study of its program. During initial meetings, the sponsor praised the open-ended question approach in the proposal. However, after the planning phase was completed and all of the site-visit schedules were established, the sponsor did an about-face and made a series of untenable demands. First, after we had carefully selected a sample, the project monitor said that she would select the sites. She nearly quadrupled the number of site categories to be included in the sample (from four to fifteen) and made numerous other sample selection requests outside the scope of the contract. In fact, the sample matrix had been altered so many times in response to the sponsor's requests that it came to resemble a multidimensional chess game. The sponsor also requested an increase in the number of sites beyond what the contract specified, but without any consideration for extra cost. Second, the project monitor wanted to change all of the questions to a closed, yes-or-no variety, abandoning the open-ended approach essential to an ethnographic evaluation. Moreover, she demanded to see all clarifying questions in writing beforehand. She did not understand that clarifying questions naturally develop during the interview situation. The sponsor also prohibited us from entering the field until we had altered our methodology to accommodate these demands. Third, the sponsor demanded that we document inadequate or inappropriate activities of sites that had already been targeted for sanctions. In essence, the sponsor planned to change the structure, scope, content, and purpose of the study design.

As director of the project, I held a number of meetings with the sponsor to attempt to respond to these concerns and arrive at a workable solution. The project monitor understood why I thought it was inappropriate and unethical to try to document sites that were already slated for sanctions and removed that obstacle from the negotiations. However, she refused to acknowledge that an increase in the sample size would require additional funds. She also remained inflexible on the subject of questions.

We reached a stalemate. The project monitor's supervisor requested a special session on the advice of their legal counsel (since the sponsor was a state of California agency, its legal counsel was from the state Attorney General's Office). I discussed the escalated stakes with my firm's senior officials, and we elected to attend with our own legal counsel. Moments before the meeting started, everyone shook hands except the project monitor, who had personalized this conflict and lost face during the previous negotiations. The sponsor threatened us with termination of the contract. Our lawyer asked that we all go back to the wording of the proposal/contract. The number of sites and associated costs were clearly spelled out in the contract. To our amazement, the project monitor's supervisor agreed with us. Apparently, a major hurdle was overcome. However, this outcome made the project monitor more defensive. She maintained her stand on the issues of open-ended versus closed questions and prespecification of additional probing or clarifying questions during interviews. Her supervisor vigorously supported her position, even though our lawyer pointed out that the contract specified open-ended questions and additional exploration into the responses of each question (with suggested probing questions in the contract). I suggested that we work on the questions together to try to reach a reasonable solution. Everyone agreed. We subsequently made a special series of (unplanned and unbudgeted) visits to the sponsor to rework the interview protocols. Unfortunately, the project monitor was not as interested in finding a productive solution to the problem as she was in reasserting her authority. During one session, her abusive language and behavior reduced one of my staff members to tears. The project monitor said that she would not bend and would make no compromise. I was still eager to make the effort productive and asked her to provide a list of closed questions that she thought might be useful or appropriate for us to pursue. She was unable or unwilling to come up with a single question. I suggested that we adjourn and start fresh the following week. She agreed, promising to try to come up with an example of what she wanted.

When my colleagues and I returned to the firm with our report of events, we learned that the sponsor had contacted our main office and initiated contract termination proceedings. Legal assistance was essential in helping us navigate through the partial termination and counterproposal, as well as claims, counterclaims, interrogatories, and the like. The sponsor reopened the issue of how many sites we would visit and refused to allow open-ended questions (while requiring an ethnographic evaluation). Our lawyer was concerned because, in keeping with my firm's policy of initiating a project before receiving any money in order to keep the project on schedule and to maintain a good-faith relationship, we had been working for the sponsor for some time but had not received any payment for our services.

At that point, it became clear that something else was going on besides a methodological difference of opinion and a power play. I decided to do a little investigative research. I made a call to an evaluator who had also had a contract with this sponsor. He in turn gave me another name. After calling several other evaluators, I had a list of evaluators who had worked for this sponsor but had never been paid. One researcher had performed all of the contracted work and presented a final draft that was accepted. Then the sponsor rejected the final report and refused to pay more than half of the costs for the entire effort. That evaluator's counsel advised him not to pursue litigation because it would have cost him more than he would have received. Another evaluator had completed all of the contracted work and presented this sponsor with a final report that was accepted and praised. However, this evaluator received no payment for services rendered. He discovered that because he worked for a state institution, he could not sue another state agency (the sponsor). Several evaluators had written proposals that the sponsor had accepted but never funded. They explained that the sponsor had used their ideas and designs to conduct its own studies and to restructure existing programs. The sponsor was thus using the proposal process to secure free evaluation services and apparently had no intention of funding any of these studies.

I shared this information with my firm's lawyers to help them document the sponsor's practices. This information was compelling and persuasive. My firm's lawyers decided to pursue the case with the support of senior management. As soon as the contract was officially terminated, our lawyer filed suit against the sponsor. The process took a number of years, and all discussions with the sponsor and the state Attorney General's Office failed to resolve the problem. Dates were finally set for various legal proceedings, including depositions. However, a week before my deposition, the state resolved the case by settlement—in our favor. We received payment for our costs, some of which went to pay legal fees. The moral and methodological victory was sweet, however protracted the fight (*Kappa Systems Inc., d.b.a. RMC Research Corporation, and RMC Research Division of Micronet Inc. v. State of California and Does 1 Through 10,* Cal. Sup. Ct., case no. 805477, 1986).

The case illustrates how useful investigative techniques can be even at a deteriorated stage in the sponsor-evaluator relationship. The techniques were not part of the evaluation per se. Instead, they were primarily used to unravel the history of the sponsor's relationships with evaluators. In turn, the information that these techniques revealed helped to persuade my firm's lawyers to pursue the case and potentially to assist in litigation (or settlement). The techniques included informal telephone calls, collection of physical evidence ranging from correspondence to legal records, and confrontational exchanges between lawyers. The telephone interviews initially allowed colleagues simply to describe their relationship with the sponsor without biasing them with my account of the problem. The exchanges were similar to regular conversations with colleagues after awards have been made to determine if there were any land mines or special client needs. In the second stage of the interview, I recounted my problem. This account typically stimulated a much more detailed and animated exchange; the real horror stories emerged during this phase of the interview. Finally, each interview concluded with a list of additional sources, both solicited and unsolicited. Documents, such as proposals and correspondence, were requested and received to corroborate the exchanges. The respondents also provided other leads, such as the names of former (often disgruntled) sponsor employees. An analysis of the legal exchanges also provided insight into the strengths and weaknesses of the sponsor's position.

Anticipation of Litigation

Evaluations and audits of suspected irregularities or problems have a relatively high probability of evolving into legal cases (see Fetterman, 1986, for a discussion of conventional, that is, non-fraud-related, investigations or audits from an anthropological perspective). The present case had all the earmarks of such an investigation. The allegations included charges that the director of a program was taking vacations with a boyfriend on company time and with company funds and was failing to report receipt of significant gifts and gratuities.

The informant (the source of the allegations) was considered credible but had no physical evidence to support the allegations. Nevertheless, the unimpeachability of the source, the past performance of the accused, and the seriousness of the charges suggested that litigation was on the horizon. Thus, the investigation proceeded with legal involvement as an anticipated outcome. As appropriate under these circumstances, a great deal of homework and scrupulous backtracking and double checking preceded every step of the investigation.

One of the first steps involved immersion in all of the director's financial records. A close scrutiny of travel reimbursement documents provided a wealth of information about the director's behavior in preparation for interviews with her. In addition, this approach enabled me to confirm one of the allegations and to identify and document another problem even before the first meeting with the director.

A review of all of the director's budget and reimbursement records revealed that she had hired a consultant to accompany her on her travel excursions. However, the consultant's address was noticeably absent on the documentation. His checks were typically sent to the director's office rather than to his home or business. A search through the records for a few prior years revealed a home address on the first check that he was issued. The director's home address was similarly difficult to determine. Although an address was listed in her personnel file, a telephone call to the residence made clear that she did not live there and had not lived there for some time. Here were two pieces of the puzzle.

An analysis of some of her other travel documents revealed that she and the consultant typically had adjoining rooms on all of their trips. This evidence was inconclusive and circumstantial. I had nothing iron-clad that linked them together at that point, so I put this piece of the puzzle aside for the moment and turned to a review of the remaining financial records, including petty cash receipts. One of the most innocuous appearing receipts in the pile, a receipt for candy, yielded an interesting piece of information. The receipt in itself was not particularly important, and the amount of money was insignificant. However, the director had listed her address on the receipt and it was the same address as the consultant's. That insignificant receipt for candy confirmed a conflict of interest between the director and the consultant. A telephone call to the county assessor to determine ownership of the residence further validated the finding. This example typifies the investigative technique of immersion. The data were meaningless in the abstract and in pieces. However, by using the allegations as a theory to guide the review and by becoming familiar with the bits and pieces of the puzzle, I was able to "know it (the evidence) when I saw it."

In the process of pursing the initial allegation, I discovered and documented another problem: falsification of travel documents for personal gain. I noticed that the consultant traveled first-class, which was against company policy. The director's travel documents for the same trip indicated that she had not flown first-class; indeed, if she had submitted tickets marked first-class, she would not have been reimbursed for the full fare. Common sense and a normative standard suggested that it was highly unlikely that the director would book a first-class seat for the consultant (whether she had a personal relationship with him or not) while she traveled in coach on the same flight. I returned to her travel reimbursement document and noticed several small marks on her travel itinerary (which she had submitted in lieu of the actual ticket) above and below the line where the consultant's otherwise identical itinerary said "first-class." Her document appeared to have been altered to hide the first-class stamp. I drove to the travel agency to secure the original, which clearly listed the director's travel as first-class. This document confirmed that the records had been altered after being issued by the travel agency and before being submitted to the company for reimbursement. (According to her staff, the director prepared and submitted her own travel reimbursement documents.) Later, the actual altered documents were found in the director's office.

Extensive preparation paid off in many other areas in the investigation. The director's immediate and unequivocal denial of both significant and insignificant facts was a useful measure of her credibility. The only area in which extensive preparation was not useful was the last allegation: the undeclared gifts. She allegedly had been receiving gifts and gratuities from wealthy clients. The allegations were extremely difficult to analyze and document. I did not have access to the clients or to their personal records.

In addition, the transactions did not go through the company system in any way. However, the fact that the director regularly dealt with diplomats from the Middle East—from cultures in which gift giving is a traditional part of business transactions—lent some credibility to the allegation. After searching for every conceivable investigative approach to address this allegation and failing to find any evidence to confirm or contradict the charge, I resorted to the old-fashioned approach of directly asking her. Rather than accuse her of receiving gifts, I mentioned that I knew it was not uncommon to receive gifts from some foreign visitors. In response, she provided a list of items, including their estimated values, their sources, and the occasions. In the process, she also indicted herself. This was the only ethical tightrope involved in the investigation. It was disconcerting to hear her answer questions with information that I knew would incriminate her. Fortunately, the other documented charges were more than enough to ensure her fate, even without this last piece of the puzzle.

Legal Maneuvering During an Investigation

In another case, a suspected irregularity actually moved into the legal domain during the investigation. In this case, the charges were that a faculty physician was violating university consulting policy, in part by keeping his wife on the payroll even though she had not appeared at work for more than four years. The latter violation was easy to document: Few supporting documents existed to substantiate any work activity during that period, and no one had seen her in the office during that period. In addition, the computer files, the office correspondence, and the wife's own retrospective reports about her work activity supported the allegation. I was asked to investigate the charges, explore relevant issues, and report my findings to the university president and the dean of the School of Medicine.

On the day that I was asked to review the problem, I received a telephone call from someone in the physician's office, claiming that the physician was discarding files. I rushed over and began to list all of the files, making notes about the contents of specific files. The employee who called retrieved some of the files from the garbage. Other employees verified that the physician was destroying files. After some probing, I discovered that the physician was destroying only insignificant files as a test to determine which of his staff members had made complaints against him. His actions were the bait to draw out the individual.

This move set the tone for the entire investigation. I returned to his office the following week to begin reviewing the records that I had catalogued. He said that I could not look at any of his (university or personal) files. I explained that I only wanted to look at the university's files, such as time records, travel reimbursement documentation, personnel appraisals, and so on. He objected, on advice of counsel. I immediately consulted the university attorneys, who agreed that I was entitled to look at university property. (A few of the physician's staff members who were concerned about his behavior kept an eye on the files in the meantime to make sure that no one tampered with them.) As soon as I received the all-clear sign, I returned to the office and began reviewing files and copying pertinent documents. Some of his staff members guided me to some troubling documents and files. I immediately photocopied those files as well as the physician's calendar, billing records, and a variety of other documents. Shortly after reviewing some of these files, I determined that they needed to be stored in a safe place. I was concerned about the destruction of sensitive files; the physician claimed that he was worried that his own staff might contaminate the files. We agreed to hold all of the documents and sensitive patient files in the university legal office for safekeeping and review.

The university documents created a useful audit trail, raising a number of serious concerns. The physician had claimed on his consulting disclosure statement that he did no consulting. However, when queried, the physician stated that he did consult but remained well within university guidelines. His travel records, calendar, billing records, and correspondence—as well as hospital incident reports—documented consulting activity significantly beyond the limits set by university policy. His calendar was filled with notes about who would cover for him during his routine absences. The calendar names, dates, and notes suggested little time for any activity but consulting. Unsolicited tips and additional telephone calls to a network of medical consulting agencies produced a long list of additional undeclared consulting activities. Comparisons between advertisements for workshops in professional magazines and his calendar, travel records, and interviews with colleagues and workshop participants identified and documented further consulting activity.

The physician never attempted to explain these contradictions. He seemed to view the situation as a game. Each time I found more information to contradict his testimony, he would accept it and say "but that's all." One of his staff members said that the physician called me Columbo (an unassuming but methodical television detective) in my absence to characterize the cat-and-mouse aspect of our relationship. A colleague described his lack of candor in the following manner: "He tells lies better than most people tell the truth." This judgment was routinely confirmed throughout the investigation. During one interview involving the associate dean of the School of Medicine, the physician, and myself, the physician gave a command performance. The associate dean asked him whether he had consulted in excess of what I had already documented and he replied no. Then the associate dean asked him if he had consulted for a specific agency, and the physician again said no. When asked if he was sure, the physician said that he never had and never planned to consult for that agency. However, through a circuitous route, I had previously found that he had in fact consulted in excess of the amount I had documented at that time. Moreover, I had received a copy of the contract from the agency with which he denied conducting consulting activity. I had discussed preliminary findings with the associate dean before the meeting, but I received the written documentation (the contract) only an hour before the meeting. I was so compelled by the physician's testimony that I had to look at the contract in my lap to reassure myself that I indeed had possession of physical documentation contradicting his claims.

After the meeting, I asked the physician why he had lied to the associate dean and to me. He asked me what I was talking about and continued to deny any additional consulting. When I described the first page of the contract to him, he said, "It must be some mistake, I definitely did not consult for that agency." When I described the second page and read sections of it to him, he maintained his innocence. I read the final page of the contract, detailing his activities, patient names, time consulting, physician's signature, and the supervisor's signature. In response to this information, he replied, "I guess you got me." I was stunned and explained to him that he had severely undermined his credibility.

The physician's lawyer had informed him that his primary concern was not his excess consulting in violation of university policy but rather my documentation of the fact that he had conducted his consulting activity on federal government property. I had entered the billing record information into a data base. One of the computer sorts was for time and place, using his calendar and corroborating witnesses to confirm the details of his activity. The consulting sanctions were relatively mild compared with a possible felony charge. His distress about that possibility led to late-night telephone calls from the physician, during which he asked me to let him know in advance if he was going to be charged with a felony. I responded that I would be happy to warn him in advance if his lawyer and the university's lawyers allowed me to communicate that information. A few weeks after his late-night telephone calls to my home, he informed his lawyer that I was harassing him by calling him late at night. This charge led to a high-powered session between the physician and his lawyer and me and my university lawyer. While his lawyer argued with my lawyer, claiming that I was harassing his client by calling him late at night, the physician interrupted to say that in fact he had been calling me late at night, asking me to call him. The physician had set up his own lawyer and then undercut him in front of the competition. In another situation, the physician said that he had stolen prescription drugs from the hospital pharmacy and was using them illegally. However, I found that again he was not telling the truth. He could not have acquired the drugs in the fashion that he described. He hoped that I would accept this negative story on face value without investigating it. Had I accepted his fabrications without further study, I would have diminished my own credibility.

During my review of his consulting activity, I also found that he had falsified medical records for his own personal gain. He had provided psychiatric consultations for well-known people across the United States. After another legal discussion, the physician and I reviewed the medical records of each of his patients. He assumed that he would be able to snow me without any difficulty. However, a number of obvious problems appeared. The records were extremely uneven and inconsistent. Diagnosed disorders and prescribed medications did not match. Patients' names were routinely crossed out and replaced with handwritten names. After a few interviews with the nurses on the ward and staff members, I was able to detect the method to his madness: He was sending his private patients' laboratory work through the hospital under regular hospital patients' names. This practice allowed him to have laboratory work done at no cost and yet to charge his private patients for the tests. The regular hospital patients would also be charged for the tests and, in some instances, the private patients' test results wound up in the regular patients' files. On discovery, this situation was corrected immediately. However, such misinformation could have resulted in misdiagnoses or mistreatments of regular hospital patients. The lawyers on both sides worked together to enable us to handle this medical emergency and greatly facilitated the correction of the medical records (see Philp and Wells, 1987, for additional details about the case in the press).

If these episodes had not been so time-consuming, emotionally draining, and potentially dangerous, they would have been amusing. At the time, they made the study even more unpredictable and difficult. Further problems posed by legal intervention included his attempts to block access to records, distractions from primary tasks, significant delays, a qualitatively higher level of personal stress, and increased investigation costs. The legal presence also sharpened the language of our exchange and constructively challenged the quality of the evidence, making the content more precise in its final form. The lawyers protected each party from the other, enabling the evaluator to pursue each lead without having to look over his shoulder at every turn, and enabling the physician to participate in the investigation without fear of continual self-incrimination.

Legal involvement in this evaluation thus had both positive and negative effects. Overall, early and continued involvement throughout the study enabled the university lawyers to make a stronger and more informed case against the individual, and continued legal involvement helped the physician to prepare and defend himself against the charges, ultimately enabling him to negotiate a more favorable separation settlement with the university.

This investigation required an endless stream of informants; myriad medical, ethical, and financial details; and rooms of files and computer data bases to cross-reference, compare, contrast, and triangulate data (Fetterman, 1989b). However, the single most important ingredient was instinct. I followed my instincts to analyze, judge, and respond to the physician's behavior and his style of playing the game. Guesses and hunches were invaluable as I followed one lead after the next, accepting dead ends and pushing forward until pieces of the puzzle came together. Months of speculation and inquiry were guided by initial allegations, informants, and bits and pieces of information and evidence. The physician's inconsistencies, games, and half-truths evident in trivial matters made me increasingly suspicious of his activities and responses in regard to the larger issues. The process of detecting his errors and violations of rules and regulations (and laws) improved after I attempted to put myself in the physician's shoes and think the way that he thought. I was better able to predict his responses and then to successfully apply that same internal logic to his past indiscretions. Instinct provided a clue and a logic for his behavior. However, each step had to be retraced and supported with physical evidence. Once again, however, instinct provided a useful tool (along with informants and common sense) in identifying and collecting appropriate and useful evidence.

Litigation in Response to Evaluation Report Findings

In a fourth case, I was asked to evaluate allegations of intimidation, cover-up, unethical behavior, legal violations, and waste and mismanagement at a major university. These allegations were made in a letter of resignation by a senior health and safety officer at the university. I spent six months on the project, conducting confidential interviews, reviewing thousands of records, and tracking down myriad leads. My public report concluded that there was substance to some of his allegations, while others were not supportable (Fetterman, 1988).

Ethical considerations were raised by a single instance in which the former employee was threatened with discharge, and many instances of mismanagement and waste were found. Some instances of the mismanagement and waste were identified by the former employee, and other instances emerged in the course of my review. However, I also found that in many cases he used terms in ways that did not conform to their general meanings. For example, the former employee had been instrumental in establishing a data base into which health and safety problems were entered; these problem lists were printed out and sent to the relevant departments for action. Frequently, there was no follow-up to ensure that the problems had been corrected. The former employee viewed this lack of follow-up as a cover-up. In this case, the data base was by no means an attempt to conceal but, to the contrary, an attempt to communicate problems to those who should deal with them. The failure to follow up is an example of ineffective institutional management: There was no systematic procedure for ensuring that identified problems were corrected (see Fetterman, 1988, for details about the study).

The evaluation required myriad investigative strategies, ranging from late-night clandestine meetings with confidential sources to following an almost endless paper trail of incriminating documents. In some cases, it was necessary to compare the testimony of expert witnesses who hated each other. Often this approach provided a common denominator of concerns that I could use as a clue or as documentation in itself. However, this study is of interest for what happened after the evaluation.

The former employee initiated a suit a few months after publication of the report, attacking the evaluation in part because of the findings. Subsequent litigation activities required almost as much time as the evaluation. The discovery phase of his lawyer's suit started with a shotgun request for documents and records. I had to review over fifty thousand lines of electronic mail, notebooks filled with evaluation documentation, and an assortment of related material to comply with the plaintiff lawyer's requests.

The lawyers on both sides argued about the relevance of specific requested documents, including some of the evaluation documentation. Confidential interview data and documents related to personnel performance were two types of data that the university counsel and I (as the evaluator) thought inappropriate to disclose. The confidential interviews were coded, and the master coding list was destroyed well before the report was released, according to normal operating procedures. However, the court could ask if the evaluator remembered who provided each interview. We also viewed personnel performance data generated from the evaluation as inappropriate and irrelevant to the case. Disclosure would have represented a potential betrayal of trust and an unnecessary invasion of privacy.

During discovery, I took part in a special meeting between the former employee and his lawyer and various university officials. The former health and safety officer presented his concerns and showed two carousels of slides of potential hazards. Many of these hazards had been remedied long ago, but he used them to illustrate his case. University officials listened and posed clarifying questions. First, the meeting provided another opportunity for the plaintiff to present his side of the story face to face. Second, university officials had an opportunity to determine whether any additional information remained to be investigated, above and beyond the evaluation report findings. Third, the exchange provided both parties with a better handle on how to proceed from that point in pretrial and courtroom strategy, including depositions and settlement negotiations.

The next major phase of litigation involved deposition. I was asked by the plaintiff's attorney to give sworn testimony for the case. He asked about my education and experience, the university, and details of my evaluation findings. I asked him to clarify questions that I did not understand. Depositions, unlike casual conversations, require precision and accuracy. I replied "yes" or "no," "I don't know," or "I don't remember" when appropriate. Whereas, under other circumstances, one might be tempted to guess or approximate answers, in a deposition such responses can diminish one's credibility to the extent that they are interpreted as a form of imprecision or carelessness. Approximate answers might even be construed as a form of dishonesty.

The plaintiff's attorney deposed me in order to gain information to build his case. My attorneys informed me that this was not the time to volunteer unsolicited information. It was the time to answer only his questions. The deposition testimony could be used to undermine my credibility during the trial.[1]

The deposition was a strenuous experience. It required tremendous concentration to be exacting and precise about every question and answer, hour after hour. The scope of the questions and the amount of material covered was mind-boggling. However, proper planning, preparation, and patience facilitated the examination and review of documents required to respond under pressure to detailed questions.

The case never went to trial: It was settled out of court, with neither party admitting fault. The plaintiff dropped his charges, and the university provided him with money and a letter of reference. Ironically, the evaluation report was in part responsible for both the litigation and the settlement. The report did not support all of the former employee's allegations, yet it provided documentation to support some of them. These findings were taken into consideration when the university decided to settle the case. Underlying this irony was the issue of cost. Right or wrong, pursuit of this litigation would have been costly for both sides. All of these influences converged to convince both parties to end the dispute.

This case illustrates how legal investigative strategies ranging from discovery to deposition provide the exact information needed to determine what happened and why and to test the quality of evaluation data and conclusions. Even the precise (albeit limiting) manner of responding to deposition inquiries provided insight into legal and investigative strategies and counterstrategies as the case unfolded. This case example also highlights some of the ethical ramifications of conducting these investigations, including the protection of confidential sources during litigation.

Conclusion

In a litigious society, evaluations and lawsuits may cross paths at any time—before, during, and after a study. In addition, a litigious atmosphere may shape the course of an investigation even without direct legal involvement. Evaluation can benefit from the rigors of legal examination and cross-examination (see Smith, 1988, for a discussion of useful concepts adapted from law for use in evaluation, including levels of evidence and adversary hearings), and investigative evaluators and auditors can benefit from the guidance and protection that they receive from attorneys. An evaluation should not be pursued in fear of litigation, though evaluators can work effectively with legal counsel to ensure that the rights of others are protected and that findings will stand up to rigorous scrutiny. Further, independent evaluation findings can shed light on a case. Investigative strategies are required to document findings in most cases of fraud and abuse. Strategies range from the mundane and methodical review of archival records to the use of a "deep throat" informant. Litigation is typically on the evaluation horizon when the stakes are high and the allegations significant. The terrain is not always smooth in an adversarial system, but together evaluators and litigators can enhance the investigation and protect the individuals involved and each other.

Note

1. The following classic legal humor was conveyed to me during my litigation preparation. A brief joke highlights the danger of volunteering information in this situation. Three peasants were about to be guillotined. The executioner led the first man to the guillotine and let the blade drop, but it stopped about an inch away from the peasant's head. The crowd judged his salvation a miracle and spared his life. The second peasant walked up to the guillotine, and placed his head beneath the blade. The executioner let the blade drop, but once again it stopped just short of removing the peasant's head from his shoulders. He was also spared and beat a hasty retreat. The third peasant put his head in the guillotine. He said helpfully, "before we begin, I just wanted to mention that there is a knot in the rope."

References

Fetterman, D. M. *Stanford Special Review on Health and Safety (Phase 2): A Report on Allegations.* Stanford, Calif.: Stanford University, 1988.

Fetterman, D. M. "Operational Auditing: A Cultural Approach." *Internal Auditor,* 1986, *43* (2), 48–53.

Fetterman, D. M. "Ethnographer as Rhetorician: Multiple Audiences Reflect Multiple Realities." *Practicing Anthropology,* 1989a, *2,* 17–18.

Fetterman, D. M. *Ethnography: Step by Step.* Newbury Park, Calif.: Sage, 1989b.

Philp, T., and Wells, J. "How Professor Fell from Grace: Stanford Career Ended Amid Federal Probe, Ethical Questions." *San Jose Mercury News,* June 7, 1987, pp. 1A, 8A–9A.

Smith, N. L. "Mining Metaphors for Methods of Practice." In D. M. Fetterman (ed.), *Qualitative Approaches to Evaluation in Education: The Silent Scientific Revolution.* New York: Praeger, 1988.

DAVID M. FETTERMAN *is an administrator and professor of education at Stanford University, Stanford, California, and Sierra Nevada College, Incline Village, Nevada. He is president of the American Anthropological Association Council on Anthropology and Education and former chair of the American Evaluation Association Qualitative Methods Topical Interest Group.*

Salient features of a modified evaluation audit and a case study evaluation are presented to illustrate two different approaches to investigation.

Audits and Case Studies: Contrasting Styles of Investigation

Thomas A. Schwandt

There are at least three ways in which the notion of "investigation" intersects with our current understanding of the theory and practice of social science research and evaluation. Several years ago, Douglas (1976) argued for a conflict paradigm of society and an inquiry posture that he called "investigative field research." Claiming that "conflict is the reality of life; suspicion is the guiding principle," Douglas called for a style of fieldwork that would allow the inquirer to penetrate the misinformation, evasion, lies, and fronts of informants (1976, p. 55). The journalistic model that Douglas explored was also examined by Guba (1981a, 1981b) as a potential metaphor for evaluation. Guba concluded that there were a number of interesting parallels both in the conceptions and in the strategies and tactics of investigative journalism and educational evaluation. Finally, in both their logic and conduct, performance or program audits (Brown, Gallagher, and Williams, 1982; Comptroller General of the United States, 1981) implicitly and explicitly endorse an investigative stance by the auditor.

Despite knowledge of these avenues of thought, my understanding of what constitutes "investigative evaluation" is more tacit than propositional. And I admit to being skeptical about identifying investigative evaluation as yet another model of evaluation when, in practice, it might be best understood as an amalgam or collage of techniques befitting Scriven's (1983) characterization of evaluation as multimodel, multimethod. These caveats aside, in the spirit of developing a "grounded" theory from the stuff that comprises our activity as evaluators, I offer here partial retellings of two evaluations in order to reveal several salient features of the

NEW DIRECTIONS FOR PROGRAM EVALUATION, no. 56, Winter 1992 © Jossey-Bass Publishers

conduct of each, thereby making it possible to judge whether each exhibits principles or characteristics of investigative evaluation. As much as possible, these portrayals remain faithful to a retelling of evaluation logics-in-use versus reconstructed logics; however, I am mindful of the unavoidable, natural human tendency to reinterpret one's own history in light of one's current thinking.

Case 1. A Training Function Review of Eastern Technology, Inc.

While employed as an evaluator with a large consulting and auditing firm, I was given the assignment of conducting an evaluation of the training division of a Fortune 500 technology company, Eastern Technology, Inc. (a pseudonym). The firm had been contracted to perform what we called a training function review (TFR), which was essentially a comprehensive study of the policies, procedures, organization, operations, and effectiveness of a training division or department (see Schwandt, 1985). The idea of this TFR arose from discussions within our evaluation and research group about the applicability of strategies of management or operations auditing and financial auditing to an examination and review of a training division's policies and organizational structure as well as to its so-called training functions (that is, planning and needs assessment, instructional design and development, delivery, evaluation, and so forth). Conceptually and procedurally, our notions of what this kind of review should entail and how it should be conducted were developing, and this engagement provided us with an opportunity to field-test our ideas and methods.

In practice, the study represented a mixture of features of case study evaluation and a clinical perspective on evaluation. For example, this study met the following definition of a case study as an empirical inquiry: "an investigation of a contemporary phenomenon within its real-life context; when the boundaries between the phenomenon and context are not clearly evident; and in which multiple sources of evidence are used" (Yin, 1984, p. 23). Furthermore, the study was conducted as an intensive, on-site fieldwork investigation. For slightly more than three months, I lived in a hotel near the site and spent every day at Eastern Technology getting to know its culture and its business, conducting interviews, making observations at meetings and company functions and rituals, examining internal memoranda and other documents, and the like. I prepared extensive field notes as well as interview notes, designed and maintained a record-keeping system, prepared interim analytical memos, and was periodically debriefed by a manager who did not have intimate knowledge of the site. All of the issues that one typically associates with ethnographic field studies—for example, gaining entry, negotiating access, developing and maintaining trust, developing a field role, managing impressions of the fieldworker, dealing with obstructive and facilitated relationships, and confronting decisions of whether or not to deceive informants (see, for example, Hammersley and Atkinson, 1983)—were encountered in this study.

However, this fieldwork unfolded within what Schein (1987) has described as an organizational development orientation or clinical perspective. As such, it exhibited the following characteristics identified by Schein: (1) The study was performed at the request of Eastern Technology and was constrained by a timetable. (2) I operated with a tacit "model" of how to improve the situation in training management and operations and to remedy problems that I identified; thus, intervention was simultaneous with data gathering and diagnosis. (3) The source and focus of the investigation was the client's systems and concerns, that is, the client initiated and sustained the investigation and terminated the relationship when it no longer chose to invest its energy and resources in the project. (4) Finally, the study was explicitly normative in orientation; it was predicated on an underlying set of models and theories about healthy, effective organizations and management strategies.

To guide my activities on a daily basis, I had a game plan that served as a heuristic device. I had prepared (as was our style in the firm where I worked) a work plan that specified the major tasks and the steps to follow in accomplishing those tasks: (1) conduct general business analysis, (2) conduct document review of policies and procedures, (3) conduct interviews with management, (4) perform preliminary analysis of key issues and concerns, (5) conduct small group interviews with division staff, (6) conduct discrepancy analysis, (7) report to advisory committee, (8) perform detailed analysis of targets and document findings, (9) prepare recommendations and action steps, and (10) conduct final review.

While the work plan was useful in pointing out the general direction in which I was headed (and, not incidentally, assuring my manager that I was accountable), it hardly functioned as a road map. Decisions about data collection (whom to interview, what to observe, what documents to examine) were made on a daily basis as the result of the previous day's investigation. Leads generated in interviews were followed up, knowledge and impressions of conditions were constantly checked against informants' views, and evolving diagnoses as well as potential change strategies were tentatively and selectively floated by gatekeepers and key decision makers. Using knowledge of organizational pathologies and diagnostic insights acquired from experience with other organizations and my interpretations of the literature in management theory and organizational behavior and change, I made decisions on the spot to abandon certain avenues of investigation as unfruitful (that is, where change was unlikely to occur) and to pursue others more vigorously. When the engagement was terminated, I submitted to the client a thirty-page technical report organized by recommendations, findings, methodology, and strategies for implementing recommendations. The report was largely a formal documentation of my efforts; that is, there was little or nothing in the report that had not been thoroughly discussed previously with the client.

The tasks of diagnosing Eastern Technology's training organization problems and developing appropriate intervention strategies were particularly difficult. The target of analysis—training division organization, management, and policies—was moving during most of my stay on-site. The organization's wants and needs were evolving as the entire organization underwent an identity crisis of sorts. It was seeking to expand into new markets while not abandoning old ones; to change its management philosophy and style from entrepreneurial to globally corporate without losing its inventive spirit, sense of family, and competitive energies; to move "up market" to compete with larger companies; and the like. It undertook three major organizational and managerial shake-ups during the time that I was on-site.

A final distinguishing feature of this evaluation is that initially I adopted the posture of a program auditor, documenting, reviewing, and attesting the existence of policies and procedures that client management claimed to have in place. The audit model of a third-party independent investigation (Schwandt and Halpern, 1988) foreshadowed the initial definition of the situation. This posture quickly shifted to that of mediator and change agent as discrepancies and problems that were uncovered demanded solutions.

That the client expected (and, indeed, required) that shift in posture is evident in the following tale: For the first several weeks that I was on-site, training division management facilitated my efforts to learn about Eastern Technology and its culture, providing me with open access to people and records. I was left alone to observe and investigate on my own, and there was no pressure from management to reveal what I had learned. The company had given me a small office on-site as a base of operations, and it was my habit to arrive there daily around 7:00 A.M. to review my plans for the day, make additional notes, confirm meetings, and so forth. Near the end of my third week on-site, the head of the training division suddenly appeared in the doorway to my office early one morning to ask, "What have you done for Eastern Technology today?" He continued to ask me that question, and I endeavored to answer it, at the same time every morning for the rest of my stay.

Case 2. A Case Study of a Staff Development Program

Recently, I was one of four case study evaluators on contract to the North Central Regional Educational Laboratory (NCREL), charged with investigating the implementation and impact of the Rural Wisconsin Reading Project (RWRP). The RWRP is a multifaceted demonstration project funded by NCREL and operated in seventeen rural school districts through the joint efforts of the local school staff, the Wisconsin Department of Public Instruction, and the Wisconsin Public Radio and Television Networks. This extensively research-grounded project was complex in its design and delivery: It was at once a rural school educational reform effort, a staff development project, a reading improvement project, and a telecommunications distance education project.

On six occasions over two school years, I spent a week or more in a single rural school district in Wisconsin investigating the implementation of the RWRP at two schools. In two separate case reports, I attempted to describe the rural school context in which this project unfolded, to tell the tale of participants' involvement and recount their perspectives on project worth, and to offer my interpretation of how the project was integrated into the life of the school district.

My particular approach in this evaluation study was grounded in Stake's (1978, 1988) notion of case study methodology and several of the premises and procedures of responsive, naturalistic evaluation as spelled out by Guba and Lincoln (1981) and Lincoln and Guba (1985). Like the Eastern Technology evaluation, this investigation relied almost exclusively on the use of anthropological or sociological fieldwork methods: formal and informal interviews with teachers and administrators, classroom and building observations, and review and analysis of project documents. It was also an on-site investigation in which the phenomenon of interest— in this case, the RWRP—was studied in situ. The activities of on-site data collection and analysis were no less intense than they were in the Eastern Technology case; however, the periods of observation were shorter and spread over a longer time frame.

Similar types of problems in fieldwork relations were also encountered, although they were of an entirely different content in each case. For example, unlike the case at Eastern Technology, where my identity and credentials as an investigator were at least partially accepted by virtue of my affiliation with the consulting firm, in the rural school in Wisconsin my credentials and role were highly suspect at the outset. At the time of my first visit to the school, I was on the faculty at the University of Illinois at Chicago, and folks in the rural school clearly expected me to be not only a university professor with little or no knowledge of the reality of schools but also, adding insult to injury in their view, a city boy who would not know a dairy cow if he saw one.

Despite shared field relations problems, the use of similar multiple methods, and the on-site nature of both evaluations, there are very important ways in which this investigation differed from the Eastern Technology study. Although I was doing neither an ethnography nor a microethnography per se (that is, I was not literally concerned with cultural interpretation or depiction of a way of life of a particular group of people [Wolcott, 1982,

1985]), I did adopt an ethnographer's posture toward the study. With respect to Schein's (1987) distinction between the clinical and ethnographic perspectives, the present case can be characterized as follows: (1) The process of inquiry was initiated by me (not by the client). (2) The foreshadowed problems that shaped the initial investigation were developed by me, not by the participants at the site, although the eventual bounding of the case was a mutual effort. (3) I was not in an action research mode, that is, I was not interested in simultaneously discovering participants' constructions of the RWRP and developing, in concert with the participants, a model for change. (4) I was far less normative in my orientation in this case; this study was not grounded from the outset in notions of organizational pathology and health. (I want to emphasize the phrase "far less normative." I believe that all social science research is normative in orientation by definition; it always reflects the value stance of the inquirer toward the object of his or her inquiry.) As opposed to the Eastern Technology case, where I felt that I had a clear idea of what constituted "healthy" organizational behavior and response to change, in the RWRP case I had less tacit and propositional knowledge of "healthy" rural schools, "effective" staff development, and the like.

The use of substantive literature in the two studies also differed. I brought to the Eastern Technology evaluation some prior knowledge of studies in management theory and organizational behavior; however, while conducting the on-site investigation, I did little in the way of additional examination of these literatures, I did not make any effort to incorporate them into my reports. In the case of the RWRP, I also was familiar with relevant related literatures as I began the study, but as the study unfolded, I did additional work, examining both empirical and conceptual accounts in the areas of staff development, distance education, and rural education. I also included some of this information in my case reports. The different approaches here are not simply attributable to a client service versus academic evaluation orientation. In fact, I viewed both evaluations as client service. The pace of the RWRP work, that is, time between site visits, as well as its setting and context, that is, an educational project evaluated under contract to an educational laboratory concerned with broad issues in rural education, seemed to require a deeper and broader perspective. I felt that it was essential to the case to incorporate certain aspects of the literature. The clinical, highly organization-specific, and action-oriented nature of my work at Eastern Technology seemed to make such a move moot.

In addition, in contrast to the Eastern Technology evaluation, this RWRP investigation placed a higher premium on description and portrayal than on diagnosis, explanation, and remedies. Informants in the Wisconsin site were concerned with the fairness and credibility of my story of their activities surrounding the RWRP. A draft of each case study was shared with the informants, who were invited to identify errors of fact and omissions, judge its overall interpretation, and so forth. Informants at Eastern Technology cared less about my interpretations than about my recommendations and action plans.

Cross-Case Commonalities

In addition to the application of qualitative methods and the posture or orientation of the fieldworker that are evident in these two evaluation cases, the following shared features warrant mention: (1) the importance of contextual analysis, (2) the response of the study to environmental cues, (3) the role of expert judgment, and (4) the moral dimension of the investigation.

Both investigations required careful contextual analysis, concomitant with an understanding of what was to be evaluated and why. In the case of Eastern Technology, this contextual analysis took the form of a general business analysis—an investigation of the organizational culture, organizational goals, and general attitudes toward and impressions of the training function within the organization. This analysis was accomplished through interviews with key management and line personnel, review of internal policy documents, and the like. In the case of the Wisconsin study, contextual analysis took the form of understanding the nature of this particular rural school, its educational philosophy, its teachers' attitudes, its role in the community, and so forth. I sought an understanding of these contextual aspects in several ways: interviews with teachers and administrators, examination of school artifacts and documents, interviews with the town's newspaper editor, informal conversations in the local restaurant, bar, and bank, and the like.

Neither study was highly preordinate in design, although the Eastern Technology evaluation did have a work plan, as mentioned above. Both studies took shape in the investigator's response to environmental cues. At Eastern Technology, I used participants' perceptions of the organization, image, and effectiveness of the training division as cues to particular aspects of the division's goals and procedures in need of attention, and as points of departure for the search for patterns. Likewise, conversations with the rural schools' teachers and administrators and observations of their daily routines revealed the salient aspects of school culture and daily existence that most influenced the implementation and integration of the RWRP.

In both studies, either expert judgment of worth or expert inference played a critical role. In the rural school evaluation, both the funder and the other stakeholders assumed that the case evaluators were experts in drawing inferences (interpretations) from the descriptive data gathered in their respective cases. The expectation was that the evaluators brought a background of understanding of the conduct of field studies, school cultures, staff development, and the like to their studies that would enable each to draw warrantable inferences from a wide variety of qualitative data. In the Eastern Technology study, I was viewed as the clinician or therapist whose expert judgment was being called on to recommend remedies for organizational problems.

Finally, both studies shared an explicit moral dimension. In neither case was I simply examining dimensions of a policy or program in the abstract; rather, I was dealing in an intimate way with people's characters, identities, and decisions about what was good for them and for their colleagues in the context of their working lives. While in neither case did I write the evaluation as a moral tale, I probably could have. At Eastern Technology, I could have told the story of how management sought to involve staff in policy-making and operations yet struggled within a corporate ethos that defined this kind of move as counterproductive to the growth of the organization. In Wisconsin, I could have told the story of how a reading specialist in the small rural district exhibited the virtue of wisdom in cautiously and gradually (rather than abruptly and precipitously) involving her fellow teachers in a new and potentially threatening innovation; how several teachers showed courage (and several did not) to persevere with an idea that they felt had real merit for improving the lot of their students, yet was not well understood by the administration and not readily welcomed by many fellow teachers; how some teachers modeled the virtue of temperance, persisting to invest much time and effort in learning about a new approach to reading without complaining that the work was not called for in their teachers' contract.

Further Reflections

The bane and boon of reflexivity is that it is endless: There are always reflections on reflections, interpretations of interpretations. Three additional reflections of concern here are the choice of the investigatory evaluation approach or methodology, the effectiveness of that approach in these two cases, and the nature of investigative evaluation.

The two evaluation situations described here did not *require* a field-based investigatory approach and attendant strategies. To be sure, the practice of acquiring familiarity with the site through on-site visits seemed necessary, but there was nothing in the nature of the situations or problems that demanded the use of fieldwork methods. In fact, what constitutes an evaluation problem, how it is delimited and cast so that it can be investigated, is itself a construction that is grounded in one's epistemological and methodological approach. The choice of methodology was driven more by personal preferences, political considerations (for example, maintenance of a high profile at the client's site in the case of Eastern Technology), and a belief in the efficacy of fieldwork methods for capturing the respondents' definitions of their situation and the importance of context. Were one to change those personal preferences, methodological assumptions, and political considerations, Eastern Technology could just as well have been investigated using some combination of questionnaires and other paper-and-pencil instruments to assess attitudes, organizational climate, and fit of policies and practices. Likewise, similar kinds of tools could have been used to gather data from the participants in the RWRP.

A complete discussion of how to judge the overall quality of the evaluation approaches in these cases is beyond the scope of this chapter. However, I can briefly point to how two attributes of quality—technical adequacy and utility—were addressed. As noted previously, a detailed work plan coupled with regular debriefings and periodic reports to client management served as means for monitoring and ensuring technical accuracy and soundness of interpretation in the Eastern Technology case. The usefulness of the evaluation was a matter of both the reasonableness and practicality of recommendations as well as respondents' views of the value of having participated in the process of the evaluation. In the RWRP case, steps taken to ensure the soundness of interpretation included the formal member checks noted earlier as well as a group debriefing conducted twice each year by all case study evaluators. Evidence of the dependability of both studies was collected through an accurate audit trail of study materials. Usefulness of the approach in the RWRP can also be gauged by respondents' perceptions of what they learned from their participation in the evaluation and how they used the case reports to change their approach to RWRP implementation.

In general, I see no reason why the standards of the Joint Committee on Standards for Educational Evaluation (1981) could not be readily applied to the conduct and outcome of the investigations. Further, in cases where evaluation investigations take somewhat different forms, the standards of the Comptroller General of the United States (1981) and those of the U.S. Department of Health and Human Services (1986) might be applicable. Another framework for judging the quality of any particular investigative strategy or tactic has been suggested by Guba (1981a). Exhibit 3.1 lists the criteria that he proposes can be applied either prospectively in determining whether a particular strategy should be applied or retrospectively.

I remain skeptical of the claim that investigative evaluation is a unique type of evaluation. My dictionary tells me that to investigate is to observe or inquire into in detail; to trace, track, and examine systematically. By this definition, all evaluation is investigative. If there is a special meaning of the term *investigative,* perhaps it is as a metaphor for a particular posture of the evaluator. What I have in mind here is neither the posture of the detective Sherlock Holmes nor the posture of the reporters Woodward and Bernstein,

Exhibit 3.1. Criteria for Evaluating Investigatory Strategies and Tactics

Need: What need did the strategy/tactic ameliorate?

Quality: Is the strategy/tactic good enough on its face to warrant its use?

Acceptability: Is the strategy/tactic likely to be acceptable to evaluation practitioners, clients, sponsors, and audiences?

Compatibility: Is the strategy/tactic likely to fit the conditions and constraints within which practitioners function?

Novelty: Is the strategy/tactic sufficiently different from already available concepts and tools to constitute a genuine innovation?

Utility: Does the strategy/tactic have sufficient promise, on its face, of working?

Cost feasibility: Can the strategy/tactic be implemented within the framework of resources typically available to practitioners?

Side effects: Is the strategy/tactic likely to be free of negative side effects and perhaps conducive of some positive side effects?

Source: Guba, 1981a, pp. 256–257.

for both conjure up images of intrigue and daring that seem a bit farfetched for program evaluators. It is more the posture of the investigator as explorer, responsive to the demands of the people and environment that he or she explores, intent on discovery.

References

Brown, R. E., Gallagher, T. P., and Williams, M. C. *Auditing Performance in Government.* New York: Wiley, 1982.

Comptroller General of the United States. General Accounting Office. *Standards for Audit of Governmental Organizations, Programs, Activities, and Functions.* (Rev. ed.) Washington, D.C.: Government Printing Office, 1981.

Douglas, J. *Investigative Social Research.* Newbury Park, Calif.: Sage, 1976.

Guba, E. G. "Investigative Journalism." In N. L. Smith (ed.), *New Techniques for Evaluation.* Newbury Park, Calif.: Sage, 1981a.

Guba, E. G. "Investigative Reporting." In N. L. Smith (ed.), *Metaphors for Evaluation.* Newbury Park, Calif.: Sage, 1981b.

Guba, E. G., and Lincoln, Y. S. *Effective Evaluation: Improving the Usefulness of Evaluation Results Through Responsive and Naturalistic Approaches.* San Francisco: Jossey-Bass, 1981.

Hammersley, M., and Atkinson, P. *Ethnography: Principles in Practice.* London: Tavistock, 1983.

Joint Committee on Standards for Educational Evaluation. *Standards for Evaluations of Educational Programs, Projects, and Materials.* New York: McGraw-Hill, 1981.

Lincoln, Y. S., and Guba, E. G. *Naturalistic Inquiry.* Newbury Park, Calif.: Sage, 1985.

Schein, E. H. *The Clinical Perspective in Fieldwork.* Sage University Paper Series on Qualitative Research Methods, no. 5. Newbury Park, Calif.: Sage, 1987.

Schwandt, T. A. "The Training Function Review: A Business Application of Case Study Research." Paper presented at the joint meeting of the Evaluation Network, the Evaluation Research Society, and the Canadian Evaluation Society, Toronto, Oct. 1985.

Schwandt, T. A., and Halpern, E. S. *Linking Auditing and Meta-Evaluation.* Newbury Park, Calif.: Sage, 1988.

Scriven, M. S. "Evaluation Ideologies." In G. F. Madaus, M. S. Scriven, and D. L. Stufflebeam (eds.), *Evaluation Models.* Boston: Kluwer-Nijhoff, 1983.

Stake, R. E. "The Case Study Method in Social Inquiry." *Educational Researcher,* 1978, 7 (2), 5–8.

Stake, R. E. "Case Study Methods in Educational Research: Seeking Sweet Water." In R. M. Jaeger (ed.), *Complementary Methods for Research in Education.* Washington, D.C.: American Educational Research Association, 1988.

U.S. Department of Health and Human Services. Office of Inspector General. *Standards for Program Inspections.* Unpublished federal document, Washington, D.C., 1986.

Wolcott, H. F. "Differing Styles of On-Site Research, or, 'If It Isn't Ethnography, What Is It?' " *Review Journal of Philosophy and Social Science,* 1982, 7 (1–2), 154–169.

Wolcott, H. F. "On Ethnographic Intent." *Educational Administration Quarterly,* 1985, 21 (3), 187–203.

Yin, R. K. *Case Study Research: Design and Methods.* Newbury Park, Calif.: Sage, 1984.

THOMAS A. SCHWANDT is associate professor in the Program on Inquiry Methodology, School of Education, Indiana University, Bloomington.

Evaluators can use criminal investigation findings to focus and design program evaluations.

Using Criminal Investigations to Improve Evaluation Results

Michael F. Mangano

In 1988, criminal investigators exposed one of the fastest growing schemes to defraud the Medicare program. Using illegal and abusive marketing and billing practices, durable medical equipment (DME) suppliers were draining millions of dollars from Medicare. Their schemes included overcharging, falsifying ordering documents, and supplying unneeded equipment. Over the next three years, investigations led to more than eighty convictions and $240 million in judgments against unscrupulous DME suppliers. These investigations also launched a series of program evaluations on the causes and magnitude of the abuses. The combined results of the investigations and evaluations helped program managers clean up these abusive practices and safeguard future Medicare expenditures.

Evaluators and criminal investigators may seem unlikely partners, but together they can produce convincing evidence for program reform. Investigators target the identification and prosecution of those who abuse or fraudulently obtain compensation from a program. Evaluators seek to improve the effectiveness and efficiency of a program—what it does and how well it does it. How can these apparently dissimilar disciplines complement each other? How can evaluators use the results of investigations to improve programs? This chapter describes criminal investigators, a case study of how evaluators worked with them to produce dramatic program results, and tips about how evaluators can work well with investigators.

Criminal Investigators

Criminal investigators include state and local law enforcement agencies, the Federal Bureau of Investigation, inspectors general, and others. Their role in relation to publicly financed programs is to identify and investigate illegal activity. They document the facts of the crime and prepare this evidence for trial. They present their cases to district, state, or U.S. attorneys for prosecution in local, state, or federal courts. Since most prosecutors have far more cases than they can handle, the strength of the evidence is a major factor in deciding which cases to prosecute.

Investigators target persons who have abused or committed fraud against a program. Abuse relates to the mistreatment of program beneficiaries or resources. For example, a doctor could sexually abuse a patient or a provider of public housing could let that housing badly deteriorate. Fraud involves illegal obtainment of something of value, such as money or other resources. Typically, fraud can mean charging for services not rendered, overcharging, or providing unnecessary services. Examples include the acts of inflating the cost of weapons sold to the Department of Defense or receiving welfare payments for fictitious individuals.

Investigators prepare cases for criminal or civil prosecution. The primary determinate is the law that was violated. Some laws are criminal statues and must be pursued that way. Others, like the Federal Civil False Claims Act, must be pursued in a civil proceeding. The rules of evidence and penalties differ for criminal and civil offenses. A criminal case requires much higher standards of proof but carries more severe penalties. In a criminal trial, the prosecutor must prove "beyond a shadow of a doubt" that the wrongdoer committed the crime and knew it was a crime. The prosecutor in a civil proceeding must prove with "a preponderance of evidence" that the wrongdoer committed the crime and should have known it was illegal. If found guilty of a criminal statute, the wrongdoer can be sent to jail, fined, and ordered to pay restitution. A person found guilty of a civil violation can be assessed damages, fined, and ordered to pay restitution, but may not be sentenced to jail.

Why should evaluators pay attention to the work of investigators? Why does it matter? There are a number of reasons. First, they both care about the good of the program. While investigators usually focus on individual cases that cause the program harm, evaluators look for vulnerabilities within the system. The focus may be different, but the objective is the same.

Investigators and their cases offer a wealth of information that can breathe life into the workings of a system that evaluators might never have the opportunity to know. This information can be helpful to evaluators in both designing a study and determining the appropriate area of inquiry. And it can be helpful in interpreting and understanding data that have already been collected.

Investigative evidence is sufficient to act on immediate cases, but it does not tell program officials everything they need to know. Evaluators can use investigative evidence and insights to help identify additional information needed, such as problem prevalence, system vulnerabilities, impact of these vulnerabilities on program operations, and possible solutions. Evaluators can design studies to get this information. The prosecuted cases of wrongdoing, moreover, can help convince program managers of the need to take action to fix areas of vulnerability identified in the system by evaluators.

Case Study of Fraud: Durable Medical Equipment

At the Office of Inspector General in the U.S. Department of Health and Human Services (HHS), evaluators work with investigators to safeguard and improve department programs. With over four hundred investigative staff, the Office of Investigations addresses fraud and abuse for the more than 250 HHS programs.

Their success is quite impressive. They achieved over thirteen hundred successful prosecutions in fiscal year 1991. Many of their case results have been used by the Office of Evaluation and Inspections (OEI) to identify and plan important new studies. The more than 140 evaluation personnel of OEI conduct rapid studies geared to the information needs of department and congressional policymakers. Their evaluation studies have brought about numerous improvements in program legislation, regulations, and operations. Here, I describe one case in which the evaluators and investigators pooled their resources and information to resolve a difficult health care problem in the Medicare program: excessive and inappropriate reimbursement of DME.

The Medicare program pays for DME such as wheelchairs, oxygen equipment, transcutaneous electrical nerve stimulators, seat lift chairs, power-operated vehicles, and crutches when they are medically necessary and prescribed for home use by a physician. Medicare requires physicians to complete a Certificate of Medical Necessity (CMN) and send it to a DME supplier. The CMN explains the need for the equipment as part of a patient's plan of treatment. One of the 200,000 DME suppliers fills the order by delivering the equipment to the patient and billing Medicare through one of its fiscal agents, called carriers. These carriers are independent insurance companies who contract with Medicare to set Medicare prices and pay their bills for a specific geographical area (usually a state).

The cost of DME to Medicare began to skyrocket in the mid-1980s. By 1990, Medicare payments for DME had increased to $3 billion. The investigators began receiving complaints from beneficiaries, doctors, reputable DME suppliers, and others that some suppliers were using questionable practices to inappropriately generate increased demand for their products, manipulate loopholes in the law, and inflate their prices. From 1988 through 1991, the Office of Investigations at HHS opened almost eight hundred cases.

The investigators uncovered a number of fraudulent business schemes to cheat the Medicare program and its beneficiaries. They included overzealous marketing, violations of the CMN, carrier "shopping," and improper use of Medicare carrier provider numbers. The investigators shared the details of these schemes with the evaluators. The evaluators learned about the specific ways DME suppliers lured unsuspecting beneficiaries into ordering equipment, pressured physicians into cooperating, obtained unwarranted provider numbers, profited from high reimbursement rates, and defrauded the program. The evaluators designed studies to determine how prevalent the activities might be and their impact on the program. Summarized below are examples of how the evaluators used the information provided by the investigators to help improve the Medicare program and reduce vulnerabilities in the system.

Overzealous Marketing and Violations of the CMN. Some DME suppliers used high-pressure sales techniques to generate consumer demand for their products. These tactics included television, radio, newspaper, and periodical advertisements that appealed directly to Medicare beneficiaries with claims of "no cost to you," or "it's your right as a Medicare beneficiary." Often, the suppliers claimed to waive—not bill for—copayments and deductibles or else misstated the real cost. All of these practices were illegal. The physician, not the beneficiary, must determine the need and order the equipment. Since copayments and deductibles are a way to limit inappropriate utilization, Medicare requires beneficiaries to pay them. Some suppliers waived copayments and deductibles after first inflating the price to cover the loss.

A more aggressive sales approach was telemarketing. Using lists of Medicare beneficiaries, some suppliers called with high-pressure sales pitches to confuse elderly beneficiaries into asking their doctors for the DME even though they may not have met the medical criteria. Alternatively, some DME suppliers asked beneficiaries for the names of their physicians. They then pressured the physicians into ordering the equipment, by threatening the loss of their patients to doctors who would cooperate.

Some DME suppliers falsified the CMNs. They did this by including additional DME not listed on the original CMNs, showing erroneous diagnoses, forging the physicians' names, or hiring their own physicians to complete the CMNs. In other instances, the supplier simply completed the form and sent it to the patient's physician to sign. The supplier did this to exert pressure on the physician to sign for something that the patient already wanted.

These CMN violations came to light during an investigation of the seat lift chair industry. A seat lift chair is a mechanized chair with a device that helps a person in standing up and sitting down. One company was running a multistate advertising blitz making false claims. They offered "free" seat lift chairs to Medicare beneficiaries. In addition to the schemes mentioned above, they often delivered the chairs before the doctors even submitted the CMNs. These chairs were repossessed when physicians would not agree to sign the CMNs, causing resentment among the beneficiaries, who would not have thought to order the chairs without the misleading advertisements.

Evaluators used the investigative findings to assess the prevalence and impact of marketing and CMN violations. They also wanted to see if system weaknesses existed that failed to preclude such activities. To get at these issues, evaluators planned national reviews of three of the most common pieces of DME: seat lift chairs, transcutaneous electrical nerve stimulators (TENS), and power-operated vehicles (POVs). The TENS is a low-voltage electrical impulse generator used as a pain-control device. Resembling a portable transistor radio, the TENS provides important therapeutic help to Medicare beneficiaries with chronic pain and acute postoperative pain. A POV is a three-wheeled battery-operated vehicle that looks like a small golf cart. It helps move patients who are unable to operate a wheelchair manually and would thus otherwise be confined to a bed or chair.

Each of these reviews included a national random sample review of Medicare claims and beneficiary interviews. Evaluators drew the samples from Medicare DME claims. They reviewed the claim records to see if the physician had properly completed the CMN with the appropriate diagnosis, justification, signature, date, and other information. They interviewed a national sample of beneficiaries to ask how they found out about the DME, how they obtained it, and what their medical condition was at the time of purchase. Finally, the evaluators reviewed a sample of Medicare carriers to determine their policies and procedures for processing DME claims.

The evaluations showed many of the same problems evidenced in the investigative work. About 40 percent of the seat lift chair beneficiaries did not need assistance in rising and sitting, and most said that they got the chairs for personal comfort. More than 85 percent of the beneficiaries said that they learned about the chairs from aggressive media marketing. Sixty-nine percent said that the supplier waived the copayment and deductible. And in about half the cases, the supplier delivered the chairs before the physicians prescribed them (U.S. Department of Health and Human Services, 1989b).

The results were similar in the POV study. Over half of the POV beneficiaries learned about them from mass advertising. Three-quarters reported that the purchase was their idea, not their physicians'. DME suppliers promised to waive deductibles and copayments in one-third of the cases. Physicians completed the CMN for one-third of the claims after the supplier delivered the POVs. Most beneficiaries said and most claims documented that they did not need the vehicles (U.S. Department of Health and Human Services, 1989a). The TENS study uncovered some of the same problems. About one-third of the claims failed to meet Medicare requirements and about 9 percent were possibly fraudulent (U.S. Department of Health and Human Services, 1989c).

Carrier Shopping. The DME suppliers submit their bills to the Medicare carrier for the state in which they are located or at the point of sale. The reimbursement rates are set by each carrier based on previous prices and other local criteria. Consequently, the same item may be reimbursed at a different rate by each carrier. As an example, for a box of ostomy kits, a supplier would get $55 in Kansas and $185 in Pennsylvania. These price differences led many DME suppliers to "carrier shop," that is, submit their bills to the carrier who paid the most. They used a number of schemes to establish a point of sale in the preferred state. The easiest was to locate an office in the state with the highest reimbursement rate. Other ways included establishing mailing addresses, telephone answering machines, call forwarding, and other devices in those states. The key was to appear to set the point of sale in high-pay states.

A good example of carrier shopping was a Texas DME supplier who commonly billed carriers in Florida and North Dakota for urinary catheters that were unneeded, unwanted, and often unusable. The supplier misrepresented the point of sale and continued billing even after the orders were canceled and beneficiaries had died. The court ordered the company to relinquish $102,000 in Medicare payments, waive their right to $800,000 in claims, and pay a civil penalty of $25,000. Thereafter, the company was excluded from participation in the Medicare program for seven years.

Evaluators sought to determine if point of sale encouraged Medicare DME suppliers to shop for the highest paying carrier and how much extra it cost the program. Their study limited the equipment to those referred to as medical supplies, a small portion of total DME. In 1989, medical supplies comprised about $409 million of the total $3 billion DME payout. Evaluators reviewed a nationally representative sample of medical supply claims and interviewed representatives of eleven carriers about their procedures for reviewing these claims. All claims in the sample were reviewed to see whether the carrier in the state in which the beneficiary resided or one in another state paid. With the use of zip code information and other analyses, the evaluators found that carriers located outside the beneficiaries' states paid about one-fourth of the claims. They then determined the difference in price for the out-of-state carrier payments versus what would have been paid by the local carrier (U.S. Department of Health and Human Services, 1991b).

The findings showed that carrier shopping for medical supplies resulted in at least $22 million in added Medicare payments. The carrier representatives supported the view that carrier shopping undermines the Medicare program through excessive payments. They said that it also increases the potential for duplicate payments by suppliers billing for an item from one carrier and then billing another for component parts. In addition, suppliers can avoid proper carrier review of the total supplier practices by spreading their billings among many carriers. Carrier personnel said that they got frequent requests from DME suppliers for their medical supply fee schedules. Suppliers used this information to decide which carriers to bill.

Provider Numbers. The investigators also pointed out major flaws in the Medicare program. Medicare carriers assign provider numbers to all DME suppliers. The numbers are used by carriers to process their claims. As discovered by investigators, anyone could get a provider number and more than one if desired. Some carriers did not even require suppliers to complete an application. They simply assigned a number once they received a claim. A supplier could also have a different number with each carrier, making it difficult to spot duplicate claims. More amazing was that Medicare systems did not identify and prevent persons convicted of prior false billings from forming new companies and getting new provider numbers.

A sample case involved a husband-and-wife team who both obtained provider numbers. They owned and operated four separate DME companies, but each was no more than a paper operation with no offices, equipment, or bank accounts. Each of the companies billed Medicare for delivering the same equipment to the same patients. Both were found guilty of Medicare fraud, sentenced to jail, and ordered to pay a large restitution.

Evaluators used case information as background to study how different carriers assign and maintain provider numbers for all medical providers, including DME suppliers. They did this in a number of stages. First, they examined Medicare law and policies. Then they obtained copies of all application forms used by carriers to get information about the provider. Next, they reviewed the documentation for a sample of provider applications to test for accuracy and completeness. The evaluators ran matches of the provider number files against state licensing offices to see if the providers were in good standing. Finally, they interviewed carrier and Medicare staff responsible for provider number assignment and maintenance (U.S. Department of Health and Human Services, 1991a, 1992).

The evaluators found a number of weaknesses in the provider number process that contributed to potential DME supplier fraud. Foremost, the carriers acquire and maintain too little provider information. One-third of the applications ask for little or no business ownership information. Ironically, carriers regulate DME suppliers the least. Often, carriers only ask for name, tax number, address, and phone number. Prior Medicare activity is absent. DME suppliers can each get more than one provider number and do business with several carriers. Carriers also did a poor job of updating their provider numbers, including failures to periodically review them and deactivate inappropriate ones. About one-half of the carriers had no formal procedures to assign or update the numbers.

Results. The evaluators and investigators presented their findings and recommendations to the administrator of the Health Care Financing Administration (HCFA), the secretary of HHS, and the Congress. The HCFA administrator manages the Medicare program. The evaluators described problem prevalence, system or program weaknesses, program impact, and potential solutions. The investigators provided the hard evidence and specific examples of how unscrupulous DME providers harmed the program and its beneficiaries. Program reform was swift and decisive.

HCFA concurred with the recommendations to strengthen the CMN process and address marketing abuses by requiring the physician to complete the CMN prior to the ordering of the equipment. The form now must show the diagnosis and reason for the equipment as part of the patient's treatment plan. The DME supplier is not permitted to prepare a form for the physician's signature or to deliver the equipment before receiving the physician's written order. The carriers are to refer all suspected abuses to the Office of Inspector General for investigation. The impact of these changes has been dramatic. Medicare reimbursement for seat lift chairs decreased from $108 million in 1988 to $500,000 in 1991. Part of this reduction resulted from the evaluators' recommendation to reimburse only for the seat lift mechanism and not the entire chair. Medicare payment for TENS units also underwent a significant drop, from $27 million in 1987 to $2 million in 1991.

HCFA further agreed to develop a national fee schedule for DME pricing and eventually reduce the number of carriers who can process DME claims from forty-eight to four. These actions will ultimately make carrier shopping moot. In the meantime, HCFA redefined the point of sale as the carrier having jurisdiction where the beneficiary lives. The provider number application and maintenance processes were also strengthened by creating a standard application requiring far more information about the supplier organization, ownership, related entities, and prior sanctions. The applicant must sign a statement attesting the veracity of all information provided, acknowledging responsibility for false or misleading statements. In addition, HCFA will require all suppliers to reenroll every two years to ensure that ownership and operating information is current. And HCFA will establish a clearinghouse of supplier number applications available to all carriers.

Tips for Strengthening Evaluator-Investigator Relationships

Over time, evaluators at OEI have learned many lessons about how to work effectively with investigators. Some of the most important are listed below. They represent ideas that other evaluators can use to establish productive relationships with investigators.

Communicate early and often with investigators. Evaluators need to get information from investigators before they can use it. Establishment of close working relationships with investigators is important to ensure continuous information flow. Communications can take many forms. Periodic visits and discussions with investigators about their cases and outcomes constitute one way. The Office of Investigations at HHS also prepares management implications reports. At the conclusion of each case, the investigator describes what implications the case may have for management. For example, a system weakness may have made it possible for the fraud to occur. Also, evaluators should give copies of all of their reports to investigators. Sometimes the issues raised in these reports relate to an investigation and cause the investigator to make a connection.

Communicate with the wrongdoers whenever possible. Evaluators can learn a great deal about program vulnerabilities from the people who actually perpetrate the crimes. Once a court has found a wrongdoer guilty, or even before, he or she may want to cooperate with investigators to receive a lesser penalty. Evaluators can ask the investigators for this information or interview the wrongdoers at a later time. This information can suggest ways to safeguard the program in the future.

Carefully coordinate investigative and evaluation work and the release of results to program officials. Evaluators should examine the work plan of investigators to learn about their special projects. Investigators are prudent with their resources and target areas that they suspect will have a high payoff. Those areas often make good evaluation candidates. Both activities can feed off and reinforce each other. The time involved in investigations through the trial period allows good opportunity for useful evaluation. The results of both investigations and evaluations presented at about the same time provide comprehensive information and maximum impact for program managers.

Learn the law and procedures for investigations. Investigators have strict policies for conducting investigations. Thus, in some cases, for example, they may not share information. When a case has been presented to a grand jury, as an illustration, investigators may not discuss the evidence with anyone. Evaluators must learn how investigators work and the rules that they must follow. Investigators will not jeopardize a case to coordinate with evaluators.

Conduct a cost-benefit analysis for recommendations. Evaluators and investigators always want to protect programs from wrongdoers, but sometimes the cure may cost more than the crime. Suggestions to safeguard program resources should save more than they cost, otherwise program managers will be reluctant to act.

Communicate often with program officials about suspected problems. When considering an evaluation, get as much information from program managers as possible about the program goals, operating procedures, laws, regulations, and the managers' knowledge and intuition about suspected problems. Find out how prevalent they believe the problems are and their reaction to potential solutions. In addition to getting their ideas, evaluators should keep program officials informed throughout the study. This approach will help them better understand evaluation and investigative findings and recommendations.

Appreciate investigators. Understand that the mission of investigators is to prevent, catch, and prosecute wrongdoers. If evaluators want their help, they will have to appreciate the extra effort of investigators. That appreciation includes courtesy and respect of their time and recognition of their contribution to the evaluation study. A mention of investigative case results in the evaluation report is a start.

Support the investigative process. Evaluators can conduct special studies for investigators, help train investigators in program areas, share information, refer potential fraud cases found in fieldwork, and other things. By doing so, they can gain the trust, appreciation, and future cooperation of the investigators.

Conclusion

Investigations are a rich but often untapped means of discovering unintended program consequences. They identify system weaknesses that fail to prevent activities harmful to program beneficiaries and wasteful of scarce resources. Evaluators can use investigative findings to pinpoint areas needing evaluation attention. The details of those criminal cases also help evaluators decide on study methodology. When evaluators combine the real-life case examples of program and beneficiary harm with their analysis of problem prevalence, system vulnerabilities, and program impact, they present program managers with a powerful stimulus for reform. Given this potent combination, evaluators should examine how they can use investigative findings to improve program results and thereby add one more approach to their evaluation tool kit.

References

U.S. Department of Health and Human Services. Office of Evaluation and Inspections. Office of Inspector General. *Medicare Coverage of Power-Operated Vehicles.* Washington, D.C.: Government Printing Office, 1989a.

U.S. Department of Health and Human Services. Office of Evaluation and Inspections. Office of Inspector General. *Medicare Coverage of Seat Lift Chairs.* Washington, D.C.: Government Printing Office, 1989b.

U.S. Department of Health and Human Services. Office of Evaluation and Inspections. Office of Inspector General. *Transcutaneous Electrical Nerve Stimulation (TENS) Devices.* Washington, D.C.: Government Printing Office, 1989c.

U.S. Department of Health and Human Services. Office of Evaluation and Inspections. Office of Inspector General. *Carrier Maintenance of Medicare Provider Numbers.* Washington, D.C.: Government Printing Office, 1991a.

U.S. Department of Health and Human Services. Office of Evaluation and Inspections. Office of Inspector General. *Carrier Shopping.* Washington, D.C.: Government Printing Office, 1991b.

U.S. Department of Health and Human Services. Office of Evaluation and Inspections. Office of Inspector General. *Carrier Assignment of Medicare Provider Numbers.* Washington, D.C.: Government Printing Office, 1992.

MICHAEL F. MANGANO *is deputy inspector general, Office of Evaluation and Inspections, Office of Inspector General, U.S. Department of Health and Human Services. He has overseen over 450 evaluation studies, given numerous interviews to television, radio, and the print media, and regularly testified before Congress.*

Investigative methods can play a role in the development of programs and policies as well as in their evaluation.

The Role of Investigation in Program and Policy Development

Debra J. Rog

Evaluation, as viewed by the authors in this volume (Smith, in particular), has become increasingly investigative. This trend is attributed, in part, to the need for evaluators to respond to the vast variety of questions, problems, and contexts posed by social and educational programs. Those who propose using investigative evaluation methods tout their flexibility in gathering information on the incremental changes in a program. In contrast to more controlled evaluation models, investigative models incorporate an exploratory stance and an ability to adapt to a program in process and in flux.

In reviewing the work of federal efforts targeted to homeless individuals, it has been observed that investigative methods also can play a role in the development of program and policy initiatives. Particularly with programs aimed at understanding and ameliorating complex, emerging social problems such as AIDS, homelessness, and drug abuse, there is often a need to act before a well-developed knowledge base is in place. Social and political pressures generally push for intervention long before there is a complete understanding of the problem that the intervention is addressing (Rog and Huebner, 1992). Thus, there is a need for rapid, incremental development of knowledge about the problem to guide the intervention and monitor its implementation.

An earlier version of this chapter was prepared while the author was employed at the National Institute of Mental Health (NIMH) Office of Programs for the Homeless Mentally Ill. The opinions presented, however, are those of the author and do not necessarily represent the official policy position of NIMH.

Evaluators have recognized the role that evaluation can play in program development, typically for individual program efforts. For local initiatives, Rog and Huebner (1992) have illustrated how interventions focused in areas in which there is little specific research and theory can benefit by drawing on existing research and theory in similar problem areas. In particular, the theory-based approach to program development has been proposed as a strategy for developing sound innovative solutions to the problems of homeless individuals. Moreover, by incorporating theory in the early stages of a program's development, it may be possible to conduct a more rigorous evaluation of the program's effectiveness and impact.

Fleischer (1983), drawing on the work of Davis and Salasin (1975), Patton (1978), and others, also described a role for evaluation in program development. Through an illustration of a case management program for low-income families, Fleischer discussed how an evaluator can assist in guiding the focus, planning, and implementation of a program. Key activities of the evaluator in this role included synthesizing and applying existing literature, participating in the actual development of the program, and advocating for use of evaluation results in the redevelopment of the program.

Edwards (1987), describing an evaluation of a nutrition program, illustrated the role of evaluation in emergent programs—those still under development. Like Smith (this volume), Edwards suggests the use of flexible evaluation models that can be adapted to the dynamic nature of a program. In particular, five attributes of emergent programs are highlighted that challenge evaluators: undefined client populations, inadequate empirical evidence linking program inputs to outcomes, shifting program objectives, treatment variation, and constraints on front-end time for program development. In these situations, a staged process of evaluation, incorporating a strong examination of the focus and implementation of the program, is advocated that can allow for changes in design to address unanticipated developments in the program and overall context.

There is virtually nothing written about strategies for macrolevel program development. Although evaluations may be conducted on large-scale programmatic initiatives such as the Robert Wood Johnson Health Care for the Homeless Program (see, for example, Wright and Weber, 1987) in which data were collected from nineteen program sites, the focus is typically directed at studying the individual programs and developing cross-cutting findings. There has been little analysis of the processes that can be used in developing larger program and policy initiatives.

This chapter, through a case study of the development of a federal program for the homeless mentally ill (Levine and Rog, 1990), suggests that a problem-solving, investigative approach may be useful for developing broad-scale policy initiatives. The example also highlights how the complex and evolving nature of the problem as well as developments in the policy area necessitated a flexible, adaptive strategy. Following the example, the chapter discussion turns to the situations that appear most conducive for an investigative approach and those in which investigation may not be the most appropriate or desired approach. The chapter closes with a discussion of the skills needed for investigative program development and a brief summary.

The Role of Investigation in Developing a Federal Program for the Homeless

Homelessness has become one of the most intractable problems of the late twentieth century. Recent estimates of the prevalence of homelessness suggest that, on any given night, the number of homeless people in the United States is between 567,000 and 600,000 (Burt and Cohen, 1989); the number of persons who are homeless during the course of a year, however, is likely to be significantly greater.

In addition to the lack of shelter, a significant portion of the homeless population experience one or more disabilities. Research has suggested that approximately 33 percent of the homeless population have severe mental illnesses (Tessler and Dennis, 1989), that at least 45 percent have alcohol problems and another 10 percent abuse drugs (Fischer, 1990), and that approximately 20 percent may suffer from both mental illness and substance abuse disorders (Fischer, 1990).

A significant segment of the present homeless population also involves families with children. The recent national shelter survey conducted by the U.S. Department of Housing and Urban Development (1989) indicates that homeless families comprise 40 percent of the shelter population, up from 21 percent in 1981. The U.S. General Accounting Office (1989) estimates that on any given night, 68,067 children and youth are homeless, and an additional 185,512 children and youth are estimated to be precariously housed. As with the single-adult population, there is growing evidence that homeless families have multiple physical health (Alperstein, Rappaport, and Flanigan, 1988; Wood, Valdez, Hayashi, and Shen, 1990), mental health (Bassuk and Rosenberg, 1988), and other problems (Molnar, Klein, Knitzer, and Ortiz-Torres, 1988). Children in particular are believed to be suffering from severe emotional, social, developmental, educational, and health problems either created or exacerbated by homelessness.

During the early and mid-1980s, however, the dimensions of the problems of homelessness were only beginning to unfurl in disparate directions. Estimates of the scope of the problem, for example, varied widely, from a federal government count of 250,000 to 350,000 on a given night (U.S. Department of Housing and Urban Development, 1984) to an advocacy estimate of three million over the course of a year (Hombs and Snyder, 1982).

There also was very little understanding of the service needs of homeless individuals and the extent to which homeless individuals suffer from problems such as mental illness, alcohol and other drug use, and other health problems. Newspaper articles and other media increasingly covered the issue, igniting concern that the problem was largely caused by deinstitutionalization.

Since 1982, the National Institute of Mental Health (NIMH) has responded to the homelessness problem by taking the lead in the federal government in identifying the mental health, housing, and support needs of homeless mentally ill individuals and in developing efforts to meet these needs (Levine and Rog, 1990). In 1988, this program was expanded and elevated to the director's office within NIMH to give higher priority to efforts directed at the problem of homelessness (Sargent, 1989).

Most of the initial efforts of this program were undertaken in an "investigative fashion." As little was known about the problem, the efforts were often exploratory in nature, driven by a problem-solving orientation rather than by a well-developed theoretical or conceptual framework of the problem. The major purpose of these first efforts was to develop a foundation for understanding the dimensions of the problem of homelessness among the mentally ill.

The NIMH program took multiple routes over the course of the 1980s, both to develop a knowledge base on the homeless mentally ill population and to rapidly disseminate this knowledge on very limited resources. These routes, described more completely elsewhere (Levine and Rog, 1990), included an interdisciplinary review of local programs across the country designed to meet the needs of homeless mentally ill individuals (Lamb, 1984); ten descriptive research studies to understand the characteristics of the homeless, particularly those who suffer from mental illnesses such as schizophrenia and manic-depression (see Tessler and Dennis, 1989); reviews of the literature on the population and mental health services (Bachrach, 1984a, 1984b) and on strategies for innovative service delivery such as consumer self-help (Long, 1988) and engagement of homeless mentally ill individuals into treatment (Rog, 1988b); "best-practice stud-ies" to identify and review emerging approaches at state and local levels that meet the needs of the population, such as intensive case management (Rog, Andranovich, and Rosenblum, 1987); workshops and conferences bringing together researchers and practitioners in areas in which little had been written on topics such as zoning (Axleroad and Toff, 1987b), mobile outreach (Axleroad and Toff, 1987a), and consumer self-help (Toff, Van Tosh, and Harp, 1988); and a clearinghouse of information to provide for more rapid and widespread exchange of information on the current state of knowledge in the field.

Thus, the early efforts were broad, aimed at building a configurational view of homelessness—a view that provided understanding of the scope and nature of the population and, simultaneously, of strategies for providing services to meet the needs of the population. Key findings that emerged from these activities concerned (1) the scope of mental illness among the population, the research indicating that approximately one-third of the homeless population suffered from severe and persistent mental illnesses; (2) the needs of homeless mentally ill individuals, who often experience multiple additional problems such as substance abuse, poor health, lack of social supports, lack of financial assistance, and lack of vocational and job skills and thus may require multiple service interventions; and (3) the characteristics of the service system, for example, the case management approach that appeared most appropriate for homeless, severely mentally ill individuals was intensive, marked by low caseloads, a flexible time orientation, and a persistent but patient style.

These findings and others derived from the multiple and diverse activities of the program during its early years helped to establish an initial foundation of knowledge. This foundation was particularly useful in guiding the framework of two mental health provisions in the Stewart B. McKinney Homeless Assistance Act of 1987 (P.L. 100-77), the first federal legislation targeted to address the health, welfare, and education needs of homeless individuals. Section 611 of the McKinney Act authorized a block grant program for services to homeless individuals who are chronically mentally ill and Section 612 of the McKinney Act authorized a community mental health services demonstration program for homeless individuals who are chronically mentally ill. The block grant program was a noncompetitive grant program designed to provide an infusion of funds to states for five services, whereas the demonstration program was a competitive grant program emphasizing the development of innovative service initiatives. The demonstration projects as well as the block grant recipients were required to provide five services: outreach, intensive case management, mental health treatment, support and supervisory assistance in housing, and management and advisory activities. Thus, the configuration of services required under both programs was informed by the emerging body of knowledge on the multiple needs of the population and the modes of service delivery exhibiting most promise.

Both of these early McKinney Act efforts, however, were limited in what they could contribute to the knowledge base. Significant questions remained concerning the extent of the problem of mental illness among homeless individuals, the determinants of homelessness, the effectiveness of services, and the most cost-effective organization of service systems.

To address these gaps in knowledge, NIMH issued a broad call for research, including epidemiological research, services research, service systems research, and research on methodological developments (NIMH, 1988). Projects funded under this call have ranged from a national survey of attitudes toward homeless and homeless mentally ill individuals to a longitudinal study of the dynamics of homelessness and mental illness in families (see "NIMH Awards . . . ," 1989; "New Research . . . ," 1990).

The NIMH research announcement has been refined recently to address additional questions arising about the homeless population (NIMH, 1991). In addition, the structure of both McKinney programs has been changed in response to increasing information on the needs of the population and to changes in the policy arena. Under Section 612, six new projects have been funded under the NIMH McKinney Research Demonstration Program for Homeless Mentally Ill Adults (see "NIMH McKinney Awards . . . ," 1990). In contrast to the early set of projects under this program, this new effort was initiated in cooperation with the Department of Housing and Urban Development; each project is designed to study the efficacy of different models of permanent housing with supportive services for severely mentally ill homeless adults. Likewise, the block grant program was replaced by Projects to Aid the Transition from Homelessness (PATH); PATH provides formula grants to states for comprehensive community mental health and support services for homeless individuals with serious mental illnesses. Thus, as the knowledge base becomes stronger, the specific methods of inquiry and intervention appear to become conceptually stronger and more refined, aimed at addressing more specific questions.

When Investigation Is a Desired Approach

Emergent social problems may demand an investigative approach, particularly in the early stages of knowledge development. As Smith (this volume) has noted, investigative methods may be most appropriate when little is known a priori about the phenomenon, when there is little control over the phenomenon, and when the phenomenon is complex and changing. The investigative approach to developing programs targeted to phenomena such as these is likely to be broad and somewhat scattered, arraying activities in a number of directions and involving multiple and various methods of inquiry. Although the overall approach may be broad, the scope of each individual activity or study is likely to be narrow. Each should be focused on a specific topic or issue in order to be implemented in a relatively tight time frame. Moreover, the individual studies should be designed rigorously and, to the extent possible, guided by a theoretical or conceptual framework. As with program development at the local level (for example, Rog and Huebner, 1992), guidance can be provided by theories and research in similar problem areas. Because the problem addressed is typically marked by a high degree of uncertainty, each line of inquiry must be of high quality in order to provide incremental evidence that can chip away at the uncertainty.

In addition, each activity should provide direction for the next set of activities. Rog (1988a) described this process as a spiraling effect in the development of a nascent knowledge base. For example, in the area of case management, the first knowledge activity supported by NIMH was an annotated bibliography. The diversity of definitions of case management led to a second study investigating best practices of case management. Results indicated that intensive forms of case management were appropriate for homeless individuals. Intensive case management was then one of the service elements tested in a first set of services demonstrations and later tested more rigorously in several research demonstrations. Each time, information developed from subsequent efforts becomes more refined, of higher quality, and more specific.

As more information is gained on a problem, knowledge development may become less emergent and more confirmatory in nature. Rather than multiple scattered routes, a few large-scale efforts may be appropriate. However, if the problem is highly politicized and/or marked by crisis periods in which acute attention is paid to the issue, it is likely that political and social pressures will continue to direct at least some of the efforts.

Investigation may work best in a program setting that supports research and scientific inquiry. A similar set of investigative methods were used in NIMH's sister program in the National Institute on Alcohol Abuse and Alcoholism (NIAAA), targeted to homeless individuals with alcohol and other drug problems. Since 1984, the program has supported multiple initiatives designed to generate new knowledge and to disseminate the knowledge. As noted by Lubran (1990), these activities have included the commissioning of literature reviews and annotated bibliographies, expert panels to guide research initiatives, and research conferences for researchers and service providers to exchange information on research and practices. The program also has had responsibility for administering Section 613 of the McKinney Act, Community Demonstrations for Alcohol and Drug Abuse Treatment for Homeless Individuals; nine grants were awarded under the first round of competition (Argeriou and McCarty, 1990), and fourteen in the second round. Cross-site evaluations as well as individual project evaluations have been implemented in each round. As with the NIMH program, as more knowledge is obtained, the specific methods of inquiry and intervention undertaken by the federal program are characterized by stronger conceptual frameworks and more rigorous methodology.

Both the NIMH program and the NIAAA program have been developed in agencies that support rigorous research and inquiry. Both are supported by staff that are trained in research and its application. Thus, acknowledgment of the critical role of research activities in the development of a program is essential if an investigative approach is to be used.

When Investigation Is Not the Most Appropriate Course of Action

Investigation may not always be the most feasible or the most desirable approach in the development of programs. The underlying logic of an initiative may be difficult to maintain if multiple lines of inquiry are being undertaken and are informing subsequent actions. Responsiveness to the needs of an issue and its development often means that a planned approach cannot be taken. Thus, goals must be broad and measures of achievement multiple. Investigation, therefore, is not the most appropriate approach in situations in which a detailed theory or conceptual framework is to be tested, the effort is short-term, goals are clearly specified and clear outcome measures are developed, a strong base of knowledge on the problem or a related issue exists that can guide the effort, the issue is clearly specified or the area is narrow, linear development of knowledge is desired, and there is no support for research or the capability does not exist to synthesize the results of the efforts as they are completed and to actively use the information in the development of subsequent efforts.

The Role of the Researcher in Investigative Program Development

Evaluators and applied researchers often can play key roles in the development of program and policy initiatives. The theory-based approach to strengthening interventions (Rog and Huebner, 1992) calls for a solid relationship between the researcher and the program planners from the initial stages of program development onward. In investigative program development, researchers may be the program planners and developers. Researchers involved in investigative development must have the ability to respond to and use the information as it is developed. Operations conducted in an investigative mode can be challenging, requiring a willingness to take a broad look at the problem and engage in and manage multiple, diverse efforts rather than focus on one or two efforts; the ability to develop program activities without a clear or well-developed a priori understanding of the problem, and to formulate and reformulate a conceptualization of the program as the activities evolve; and the ability to analyze the information as it is collected to determine if other courses of action are warranted and desirable, and to respond rapidly to put these courses of action into place.

Conclusion

Investigative program development may be particularly warranted for programs targeted to emerging, complex, and dynamic social problems. Through an illustration of the development of a federal program focused on the needs of the homeless mentally ill population, I have examined here how investigative methods can be used to develop a strong base of knowledge as a foundation for further research and service efforts.

References

Alperstein, G., Rappaport, C., and Flanigan, J. "Health Problems of Homeless Children in New York City." *American Journal of Public Health,* 1988, 78, 1232–1233.

Argeriou, M., and McCarty, D. (eds.). *Treating Alcoholism and Drug Abuse Among Homeless Men and Women: Nine Community Demonstration Grants.* New York: Haworth Press, 1990.

Axleroad, S. E., and Toff, G. E. *Outreach Services for Homeless Mentally Ill People.* Rockville, Md.: National Institute of Mental Health, 1987a.

Axleroad, S. E., and Toff, G. E. *Zoning Issues in the Development of Housing for Homeless Persons Who Are Mentally Ill.* Rockville, Md.: National Institute of Mental Health, 1987b.

Bachrach, L. L. *The Homeless Mentally Ill and Mental Health Services: An Analytical Review of the Literature.* Washington, D.C.: Government Printing Office, 1984a.

Bachrach, L. L. "The Homeless Mentally Ill and Mental Health Services: An Analytical Review of the Literature." In H. R. Lamb (ed.), *The Homeless Mentally Ill: A Task Force Report of the American Psychiatric Association.* Washington, D.C.: American Psychiatric Association, 1984b.

Bassuk, E. L., and Rosenberg, L. "Why Does Family Homelessness Occur? A Case-Control Study." *American Journal of Public Health,* 1988, 78, 783–788.

Burt, M. R., and Cohen, B. E. *America's Homeless: Numbers, Characteristics, and Programs That Serve Them.* Washington, D.C.: Urban Institute Press, 1989.

Davis, H. R., and Salasin, S. E. "The Utilization of Evaluation." In E. L. Struening and M. Guttentag (eds.), *Handbook of Evaluation Research.* Vol. 1. Newbury Park, Calif.: Sage, 1975.

Edwards, P. "Conceptual and Methodological Issues in Evaluating Emergent Programs." *Evaluation and Program Planning,* 1987, 10, 27–34.

Fischer, P. *Alcohol and Drug Abuse and Mental Health Problems Among Homeless Persons: A Review of the Literature, 1980–1990.* Washington, D.C.: National Institute on Alcohol Abuse and Alcoholism, 1990.

Fleischer, M. "The Evaluator as Program Consultant." *Evaluation and Program Planning,* 1983, 6, 69–76.

Hombs, M. E., and Snyder, M. *Homelessness in America: Forced March to Nowhere.* Washington, D.C.: Community for Creative Nonviolence, 1982.

Lamb, H. R. (ed.). *The Homeless Mentally Ill: A Task Force Report of the American Psychiatric Association.* Washington, D.C.: American Psychiatric Association, 1984.

Levine, I. S., and Rog, D. J. "Mental Health Services for Homeless Mentally Ill Persons: Federal Initiatives and Current Service Trends." *American Psychologist,* 1990, 45, 963–968.

Long, L. *Consumer-Run Self-Help Programs Serving People Who Are Homeless and Mentally Ill.* Vols. 1–3. Rockville, Md.: National Institute of Mental Health, 1988.

Lubran, B. "Alcohol and Drug Abuse Among the Homeless Population: A National Response." In M. Argeriou and D. McCarty (eds.), *Treating Alcoholism and Drug Abuse Among Homeless Men and Women: Nine Community Demonstration Grants.* New York: Haworth Press, 1990.

Molnar, J., Klein, T., Knitzer, J., and Ortiz-Torres, B. *Home Is Where the Heart Is: The Crisis of Homeless Children and Families in New York City.* [Report] New York: Edna McConnell Clark Foundation, 1988.

National Institute of Mental Health (NIMH). *Research and Research Demonstrations on Homeless Severely Mentally Ill Adults and Homeless Families with Children Who Are at Risk of Severe Emotional Disturbance.* Rockville, Md.: NIMH, 1988.

National Institute of Mental Health. *Mental Health Research on Homeless Persons.* Rockville, Md.: NIMH, 1991.

"New Research Will Focus on Homeless Families and Mentally Ill Adults." *Access,* Sept. 1990, p. 4.

"NIMH Awards $3.1 M to Study Homeless Mentally Ill." *Access,* Sept. 1989, p. 1.

"NIMH McKinney Awards Total $5.3 Million for Housing and Services." *Access,* Sept. 1990, p. 1.

Patton, M. Q. *Utilization-Focused Evaluation.* Newbury Park, Calif.: Sage, 1978.

Rog, D. J. "Improving Service Delivery to Homeless Mentally Ill Persons Through Improvements in the Knowledge Base." Paper presented at the annual meeting of the Howard R. Davis Society for Knowledge Utilization and Planned Change, Chicago, Nov. 1988a.

Rog, D. J. *Engaging Homeless Persons with Mental Illness into Treatment.* Rockville, Md.: National Institute of Mental Health, 1988b.

Rog, D. J., Andranovich, G. D., and Rosenblum, S. *Intensive Case Management for Persons Who Are Homeless Mentally Ill: A Review of Community Support Program and Human Resource Development Program Efforts.* Rockville, Md.: National Institute of Mental Health, 1987.

Rog, D. J., and Huebner, R. "Using Research and Theory in Developing Innovative Programs for Homeless Individuals." In H. T. Chen and P. Rossi (eds.), *Theory-Driven Evaluation: Analyzing and Developing Programs and Policies.* Westport, Conn.: Greenwood, 1992.

Sargent, M. "Update on Programs for the Homeless Mentally Ill." *Hospital and Community Psychiatry,* 1989, *40,* 1015–1016.

Tessler, R. C., and Dennis, D. L. *A Synthesis of NIMH-Funded Research Concerning Persons Who Are Homeless and Mentally Ill.* Rockville, Md.: National Institute of Mental Health, 1989.

Toff, G. E., Van Tosh, L., and Harp, H. "Self-Help Programs Serving People Who Are Homeless and Mentally Ill." In G. E. Toff (ed.), *Proceedings of the Fourth Knowledge Development Meeting on Issues Affecting Homeless Mentally Ill People.* Washington, D.C.: Intergovernmental Health Policy Project, George Washington University, 1988.

U.S. Department of Housing and Urban Development. *A Report to the Secretary on the Homeless and Emergency Shelters.* Washington, D.C.: Government Printing Office, 1984.

U.S. Department of Housing and Urban Development. *A Report on the 1988 National Survey of Shelters for the Homeless.* Washington, D.C.: Government Printing Office, 1989.

U.S. General Accounting Office. *Children and Youths: About 68,000 Homeless and 186,000 in Shared Housing at Any Given Time.* Washington, D.C.: Government Printing Office, 1989.

Wood, D., Valdez, B., Hayashi, T., and Shen, A. "Health of Homeless Children and Housed, Poor Children." *Pediatrics,* 1990, *86,* 858–866.

Wright, J., and Weber, E. *Homelessness and Health.* New York: McGraw-Hill, 1987.

DEBRA J. ROG *is research fellow with the Washington, D.C., office of the Vanderbilt Center for Mental Health Policy, and assistant research professor of public policy at Vanderbilt University, Nashville, Tennessee. Her current research and work involves homelessness, housing, and the development of applied research methods.*

Evaluation in international technical assistance programs places a unique set of pressures on the evaluator, which in turn places special demands on the investigative strategies employed.

Investigative Strategy in International Technical Assistance Projects

David W. Chapman

Most nonmilitary foreign aid to developing countries is awarded to fund specific development projects managed by the recipient government, by a donor agency, or by a development contractor. The question of how to allocate aid funds across competing sectors—health, agriculture, community development, and education—or among priorities within a single sector is under continuous deliberation and debate. Increasingly, program evaluators are being asked to participate in these deliberations as donors and recipient government officials come under pressure to demonstrate that the interventions they sponsor are effective, efficient, and well received by the target audience—in short, that the funds have been wisely used. While an interesting and potentially important context for evaluation, evaluation in international technical assistance programs places a unique set of pressures on the evaluator which, in turn, places special demands on the investigative strategies employed. This chapter reflects on the investigative strategies often employed in the evaluation of international technical assistance programs and presents a six-element approach particularly appropriate for evaluation activities at the project planning stage.

The choice of an appropriate investigative strategy has much to do with the role in which evaluation is employed in a program. There is a paradox in the role of evaluation in international technical assistance projects: The clearest mandate for evaluation (a summative role) would have it occur

Appreciation is expressed to Kathleen Toms for her helpful thoughts on the similarity of detectives and evaluators.

after its point of maximum usefulness (a formative role). Yet, despite its potential usefulness in a formative role, evaluation is seldom employed that way in development assistance programs. The place where evaluation *is used* and *does* have an important impact is at the planning and project formulation stage. Evaluation in these roles is investigative rather than confirmatory, and its purpose is to uncover events, contingencies, and relationships that will shape, facilitate, or constrain movement toward larger development objectives. It is in the service of designing an intervention rather than ascertaining its impact. However, the investigative strategies employed at this early stage pose special challenges to the evaluator. To understand the argument for the needs assessment role of evaluation, it is necessary first to understand why process and product evaluation have been so poorly received.

Evaluation in Education Development
Assistance Projects

Donor-funded international programs normally mandate formal evaluation in a summative role to render a judgment of success or failure at the conclusion of a project. Often such information comes too late to assist the present project, and its contribution to subsequent large-scale technical assistance is limited. Few of these large-scale projects are ever replicated (at least in a way that could benefit from previous evaluations). Even in the consideration of continuation of funding, project managers and government officials need to commit to continuation (or redesign) long before summative data about the earlier project cycle are available.

While ongoing evaluation in a formative role would appear to be a more useful focus of evaluation effort, international technical assistance programs tend to overlook or minimize evaluation in this role. Alterations of crucial commitments and contracts to solve midcourse problems often are difficult insofar as they require considerable justification and extra work and raise questions at higher administrative levels about the adequacy of the initial planning process. Formative evaluation may be ignored because of a tacit belief by program managers that adherence to the original plan, even if flawed, is preferable to undertaking changes that either may reflect poorly on the initial plan (and the planners) or appear to change project costs once financial agreements have been negotiated.

The net result of these constraints on the usefulness of formative evaluation is the placement of even greater importance on the quality, integrity, and wisdom that go into the design of interventions in the first place. This has forced evaluation away from a retrospective confirmatory role toward a more proactive investigative role. The most useful role for evaluation is at the needs assessment and project design stages, since work at those points can shape how funds are spent and how programs are designed. This early role for evaluation has become more pronounced in the last ten years due to two trends in development planning. The first is the shift away from single-problem-oriented interventions and toward sectoral and cross-sectoral strategies. The second is the shift from problem-focused lending to policy adjustment lending.

Shifting Patterns of Development Assistance Funding

The conventional approach to international technical assistance has been project-oriented. A development problem was identified and isolated—for example, a shortfall of trained teachers, inadequate materials distribution to the schools, or a shortage of electricity in a particular area—and a potential solution was designed in the form of a targeted project. The trouble was that these projects often failed to have the anticipated impact and frequently, in the effort to solve the target problem, other equally serious problems were created. These failures were not necessarily because the projects were poorly targeted or badly implemented but because planners failed to recognize the sectorwide implications of the intervention.

This move to sectoral planning is grounded in systems theory. Systems theory posits that subsystems are interrelated and that changes to any one subsystem have consequences for other subsystems. Good project planning needs to anticipate both the concurrent activities in other parts of the sector that must occur if the target intervention is to succeed and, in turn, how successful achievement of the target project will alter relationships, incentive systems, and practices in other parts of the sector. Sector-focused interventions, then, are designed to simultaneously address several key issues within a sector, thereby improving the prospects of project success and sustainability. Needless to say, as development planning follows a more sectorwide approach, cross-linkages within and among sectors (and the job of identifying appropriate development interventions) become exponentially more complex.

Along with the shift to sector and cross-sectoral project planning is the shift from problem-focused lending to a policy adjustment lending strategy. Development assistance funding increasingly is being tied to larger policy issues—the promise of funding in one area is used as leverage to exact policy and procedural changes in other areas (Habte and Fuller, in press). Advocates argue that this trend results in greater payoff for the funds invested. Critics argue that planners and policymakers often have an inadequate understanding of the impacts on school practice of the policies that they are trying to effect. Some advocates counter that these relationships should be investigated as part of the project identification and formulation stage. The move toward policy adjustment lending further increases the importance of sector-level analytical skills for those involved in needs assessment and project planning.

Consequently, the evaluator's role in needs assessment goes well beyond the determination of the need for a particular intervention, the review of the logical consistency of a proposed plan, or the analysis of its relevance within a particular context. The emphasis of needs assessment and planning is on identifying the central development issues and the key links among development issues in ways that inform the planning of sectorwide interventions.

These trends have three specific implications for education development planning. First, technical assistance has to be more fully integrated with applied policy research to help anticipate and plan for sectoral and cross-sectoral impacts. Second, staff involved with this more complex policy adjustment and sectoral educational development strategy need to have a different (and, in many ways, more sophisticated) set of interpersonal, diplomatic, and technical skills than are needed for planning single-problem interventions. They must operate from a broader, more complicated understanding of the educational and national development process. Third, mistakes in sectoral and cross-sectoral planning are more expensive than mistakes within single-problem projects. The more complex approach requires that more attention be given to building on the experience of earlier projects.

Contextual Factors That Shape Selection of Investigative Strategy

These trends shape the needs assessment and project planning tasks, which, in turn, shape the investigative strategies that can be used. However, these investigative strategies are further shaped by the particular context in which the inquiry is conducted. This section examines five contextual factors that influence investigative strategies in the settings of developing countries.

The availability of relevant data is limited and the quality of available data often is low or unknown. Developing countries generally do not have a strong tradition of data-based decision making. One result is that data frequently are not available. Decisions are more often based on personal experience, family or tribal loyalties, or political considerations. Even where data bases exist, they tend to emphasize descriptive information about the current status of the education system rather than projections of future needs. Further, the data that do exist often are of low or unknown quality. In many countries, the convergence of poor communications, weak administrative systems, and inadequate numbers of staff trained in data analysis tends to undermine the accuracy and usability of the data collected.

Even where national data are available at a seemingly reasonable quality level, local decision makers may be highly dubious about their accuracy. Sometimes this is a correct assessment grounded in their understanding of how data are collected and transferred from schools to the ministry. At other times, the assessment is a reflection of their own limits in understanding how to use data. Recent research on data quality in developing countries indicates that ministry officials and educators tend to hold substantially inaccurate judgments about the quality of national education data, but in ways that defy easy generalizations across countries (Imboden, 1980; Chapman and Dhungana, 1989; Chapman, Gaal, Burchfield, and Messec, 1989). For example, officials in Nepal tend to underestimate the quality of their national education data, whereas officials in Yemen tend to overestimate the quality of their data (Chapman and Boothroyd, 1988b; Chapman, 1989). The evaluator must not only locate available data but also make a series of judgments about the quality and usability of those data. More important, the evaluator must have the skill, confidence, and chutzpah to make inferences on less data than are typically available in more developed countries.

The technical skills of many key decision makers are limited by inadequate training, in turn constraining the types of analyses that the consultant can use effectively. Inferential statistics generally are not well understood. Government officials and educators often lack training in interpreting or using inferential statistics and frequently do not understand arguments grounded in those types of statistics. The problem posed by using inferential data is far more serious than the creation of simple misunderstandings. The use of analytical techniques that are not understood smacks, at worst, of a foreign plot to subvert local prerogatives. At best, decision makers are placed in the position of defending decisions with arguments that they do not fully understand.

Operationally, this circumstance limits much of the consultant's recourse to statistical tools to basic arithmetic procedures such as the computation of ratios and trends. Recommended interventions must be advanced in terms of relatively straightforward treatment of available evidence.

The evaluator is working in a setting in which many subtle relationships and processes are unknown. Some of the problems of conducting a needs assessment in another culture are similar to the problems encountered in reading a detective novel in translation. An American reading an English version of a French detective story may understand each clue as it is offered but totally miss the connections among them that a Frenchman would immediately grasp. The foreigner lacks the richer context within which to identify an event as a clue or interpret its real significance.

This limited awareness is an inherent aspect of working in a foreign culture. The issue goes beyond the limitations of linguistic or cultural familiarity. Power relationships, patterns of information flow, and access to resources often follow familial, tribal, or political lines that may be invisible to an outsider—even an outsider with substantial in-country experience. People's informal power will often differ from their formal position within the organization, a factor not easily observed by consultants who have only limited history or contact with these personnel. It is unlikely that a consultant will develop a full grasp of these dynamics or will understand the subtler aspects of the linkages that hold certain patterns of behavior in place while allowing others to be easily altered.

These complex and all-but-invisible relationships can act as a semipermeable membrane, selectively filtering the nature and quality of information that flows to the consultant. Investigative strategies, then, must be similar to newspaper reporting—information must be confirmed by independent sources before too much is done with it. A second appropriate response to the filter effect is to increase the grounding of recommendations in empirical data in order to establish a more objective basis for discussions among potentially competing constituents.

The assessment of needs is conducted in a complex political environment. Often, the environmental context of the evaluation is marked by sharp differences in the political and economic power wielded by various constituent groups interested in the eventual programming of donor funds. Although a familiar characteristic of evaluation contexts, this power differential is probably a matter of degree rather than of nature. Decision making in many developing countries still operates within an essentially totalitarian framework, in which opposition is poorly tolerated. The disparities in power between those in and those not in power can be enormous, with dissension unwelcome.

The obvious challenge to the evaluator is to accurately reflect the interests of all key groups in the assessment. This task is easier said than done, especially given the problems of correctly determining those interests. The self-interest of any given group may not be what it appears to a consultant. The rational self-interest of an individual may be best served by supporting what is, by any objective measure, an inefficient system or procedure, particularly when the individual is in a position of sufficient power in the organization to exploit the system inefficiencies for his or her self-interest. Good innovations may fail not because they are poorly targeted, badly designed, or improperly implemented but rather because they do not provide adequate incentives to hold the participation of key people and groups. Effective changes are those that adequately address the incentive systems that hold existing patterns of behavior in place.

The evaluator seldom knows beforehand what data will be available. In some respects, limited prior knowledge about available data characterizes most evaluation consultancies. The main difference is that an international technical assistance team usually only has four to six weeks to assess the situation; collect, analyze, and draw conclusions from existing data; and represent those conclusions in negotiations with recipient government personnel. The investigative strategies of the evaluator need to include a blueprint for rapid examination and manipulation of existing data, which requires the evaluator to have a firm grounding in indicators of educational quality and efficiency. The consultant must operate from an existing template of concepts, definitions, and approaches that allows for the rapid organization of what otherwise can be an overwhelming amount of data. This mental template is not a subjective creation of the evaluator but rather is solidly grounded in the literature and experience of international development. Just as detectives need to know the most current forensic techniques for examining evidence, evaluators must be familiar with the most current techniques for organizing information and identifying clues from the data available to them.

Investigative Strategy

The investigative strategy most effectively employed at the needs assessment and project planning stages of international development planning emphasizes six characteristics:

Data-Based Analysis. An essential element in sector-level analysis of needs is a firm foundation of empirical data; quantitative data play an important role here even though these data may be of questionable quality. Objective data serve as a focal point of discussion among parties who may operate with different interests and beliefs about what happens in the education sector. If the assertion of issues, problems, and needs is presented in terms of locally collected data, then disagreements about a particular conclusion must be based on considerations of the data quality or the manner in which the data were used to support the proposal under consideration. Data do not necessarily drive decisions, but they can inform the debates that lead to those decisions, and sometimes they can be used to constrain bad decisions made on less objective grounds. An essential role of the consultant is to establish a framework within which policy and planning discussions can proceed in a productive way. An important investigative strategy of the consultant, then, is to make maximum use of the quantitative data available in formulating conclusions and recommendations.

The evaluator must recognize "clues" within the data, presenting the data in such a way that others can also see the clues, and suggesting the larger pattern and issues toward which the clues point. Sometimes these clues concern the trends and relationships that are observed in the data; other times they concern the discrepancies among quantitative data collected from different sources. Often they emerge from the discrepancy between what "witnesses" report and what the quantitative data suggest.

Two strategies tend to have high payoffs in consultants' efforts to ground evaluations in empirical data. First, the lack of communication within and across ministries that typifies developing countries means that more data relevant to the issues at hand may be available than personnel in any particular unit realize. To the extent that consultants working at the sector level can combine data from these different local sources, they often can formulate recommendations that offer new insights to local decision makers. Second, consultants often can show local personnel how to use existing data in different ways by operationalizing new indicators of educational quality and efficiency. For example, in an education sector assessment in Botswana, the assessment team discovered that community-financed junior secondary schools were being encouraged by the government, in large part because the *unit cost* of educating students in these schools was lower than the alternative types of schooling available to them. However, using data already available in the ministry, the assessment team was able to show that the *cycle cost* for community-based junior secondary schooling was actually higher than other alternatives. While per pupil costs were indeed lower, costs to produce a graduate were higher due to the high rate of attrition that characterized these schools (Government of Botswana, 1984).

Use of Key Informants. Local educators and government officials generally know the central problems of their education system, and many have good ideas for how those problems can be resolved. Indeed, local informants are the key to effective needs assessment, since few consultants are in a position to know either the issues or the relationships among issues that define the opportunities of and constraints on an education system.

There are pitfalls, however, in using key informants. The most common problem is the confusion of language fluency for insight and sincerity. A less experienced consultant may tend to rely on key informants because they can express themselves well in the consultant's language, though they may fail to capture the insights and points of view of those with whom it is more difficult to communicate. A second problem is that in the face of substantial amounts of development assistance monies, many informants have a vested interest in shaping the flow of those funds. Their "insights" are often self-serving and need to be evaluated within a larger context of conflicting needs and priorities.

To help compensate for these disadvantages, the evaluator must operate like a detective. The investigative strategy of both evaluator and detective relies heavily on comparisons of key informant interviews with other types of data that the investigator collects. The storybook detective may ask questions such as, Could he have killed her and still made the station in time for the 12:15 to London, arriving in time for the dinner party that is his alibi? The evaluator designing a development project is more likely to ask if in-service training could work, given that roads are impassable for six months a year during the rainy season, or whether teachers would attend training when they hold second jobs that conflict with the training time. Nonetheless, there is a similarity in the methods of detectives and evaluators: collection of evidence from multiple sources, examination of the consistency across that evidence, recognition of clues, and formulation of hypotheses to be confirmed (or disconfirmed) through the collection of yet further information. In both cases, the emphasis is on discovery, on uncovering the unknown.

Indicators of Educational Effectiveness and Efficiency. A necessary starting point in needs assessment is the identification of a core set of education indicators around which consensus already exists or can quickly be built. Yet, given the disagreement and debate in highly industrialized countries about what constitutes appropriate indicators of education quality and efficiency, it should come as no surprise that education leaders in many developing countries have given little attention to the issue and that little or no consensus exists. Many countries lack a clear set of indicators with which to gauge educational progress or efficiency (Alkin, 1988; Windham, 1988).

Consultants' ability to assess sector needs depends heavily on the extent to which they can quickly introduce and operate from a set of indicators that will have credibility and acceptance. For the consultant, this set of indicators operates as a conceptual framework within which events, information, and evidence can be organized. For the country constituent groups, these indicators help focus attention that could otherwise be directed toward less important issues. Further, these indicators of educational progress and efficiency often end up serving as the criteria employed in subsequent product evaluations.

Rapid Appraisal Methodology. Investigative strategies are easily bogged down by either too little data, leaving the evaluator unsure of how to proceed, or too much data, leaving the evaluator buried in information. The evaluator must make quick decisions about what things are worth knowing, what things can be ignored, and the level of specificity necessary for those things worth knowing. Many planning decisions require that planners understand the direction and general magnitude of a problem. Additional time spent on refining estimates of the magnitude of a problem is often time wasted. A balance must be sought between the cost of collecting and ensuring the accuracy of data versus the potential cost of basing decisions on inaccurate data (Chapman and Boothroyd, 1988a, 1988b). Many planning decisions do not require high levels of precision; decision makers need only to understand the direction and general magnitude of trends. If, as in the case of Liberia, primary school enrollments have dropped dramatically in the last four years, it is probably not important whether it was a 20 or a 25 percent drop—the policy implications are the same (Government of Liberia, 1988).

These pressures require that the evaluator employ a rapid appraisal methodology. Rapid appraisal methodology is grounded in the recognition that not all potentially relevant information contributes to improving the decision, not all information is eventually relevant or worth knowing (Chambers, 1981). Under pressures of time, it may be necessary and appropriate to trade off comprehensiveness of data for timeliness of decision. The method is particularly suited to planning situations in which decisions are forced by time lines that cannot be stretched to accommodate additional analysis of marginal value to the decision at hand. In a rapid appraisal approach, the evaluator must judge, first, what data are worth knowing, and, second, for those data worth knowing, what level of accuracy is necessary.

Cross-Unit Impacts. A common observation across developing countries is that administrative units are largely self-contained and autonomous, lacking strong coordination, even with other units in the same ministry. In such situations, there is little or no sharing of information across administrative units. Relationships are characterized as more competitive than collaborative. Information is withheld as a means of enhancing the stature and importance of a unit. Often, no one is responsible for analyzing the cross-impacts of activities undertaken within the same ministry. Consequently, one of the highest payoff strategies in assessing sector needs is the analysis of the cross-impacts of activities undertaken by the various units of the same ministry. It frequently shows that ministry actions are operating at cross-purposes.

The investigative dimension of this analysis resides in the need to get access to data that unit managers prefer to keep in their own domain of control and, second, in the manner in which the evaluator combines those data with information from other sources to reach new insights and conclusions that shape the design of development activities. While the merging of cross-unit and cross-sector data can offer dramatic new understandings, those insights might come at the expense of key actors feeling exposed or resentful over the loss of exclusive control over information. Unlike criminal investigators, who may not care whose sensitivities they offend, evaluators have to care. The success of an eventual program may depend on the support of those same unit managers; investigative strategies cannot antagonize the very people on whom the subsequent project success may depend. Investigative technique, then, involves seeking out information that may not be readily shared, but in a manner that minimizes the antagonism of key actors.

Sector Focus. How one analyzes a specific problem in education development is far more widely understood than how one analyzes the needs of an entire sector of the economy. Considerable progress has been made in the last five years in formulating and testing a sector assessment methodology that appears to be effective across a wide variety of settings and stages of development (Improving the Efficiency of Education Systems Project, 1989). Within the most commonly used sector assessment methodology, the potential for development of the education sector is analyzed in terms of the fiscal capacity of government, manpower supply and demand, education cost and financing, and the management capacity of government in general and within the education sector in particular. Then, each subsector of the education system is examined in terms of external efficiency, internal efficiency, cost and financing, administration and supervision, and access and equity (Pigozzi and Cieutat, 1988). This analysis is the basis for a set of recommendations for continued development of each subsector within the constraints posed by the development needs of the overall sector. This type of schema is essential to an efficient investigative strategy. Without it, the complexity of sector-level planning can quickly become overwhelming.

Specific organizational issues that need attention often are readily evident, for example, low teacher qualifications, high student attrition, and an inadequate system for distributing educational material. The greater challenge is in detecting how these issues are woven together in order to design more comprehensive interventions that address several issues simultaneously. The evaluator must examine events from multiple frameworks—to explore not just the sector-specific impacts of activities but also the wider economic, political, and cultural impacts of any proposed change. While a content knowledge in the sector is helpful, it is not at all sufficient. The ability to analyze complex relationships, to discern patterns, and to understand cross-impacts among activities are essential skills.

Conclusion

The most important role of evaluators in international development assistance programs often occurs before a program is even implemented, at the needs assessment and planning stage. One implication of this timing is a shift in emphasis from confirmation (Did a program work? Did participants like it?) to an emphasis on investigation (What type of intervention best addresses the multiple needs of the education sector?). Moreover, the settings in which these evaluative investigations are conducted place severe demands on the particular investigative strategies that evaluators can employ. Constraints of time, data quality, technical sophistication of key audiences, and the sheer complexity introduced by a cross-unit or cross-sector orientation impose pressures on the evaluator that are different from those encountered in many domestic settings.

While evaluators, as a group, often lament the limited impact of their work on subsequent program and funding decisions, some take private consolation in the fact that this exclusion limits their responsibility and liability for the misjudgments committed by program planners and administrators. Evaluators in international development planning, just as their counterparts in domestic evaluation activities, are sometimes ignored.

However, the more awesome experience is that their recommendations are sometimes heeded. Their recommendations can directly shape the programming of millions of dollars of donor and government funding; their work may have direct influence on the amount and quality of the education received by thousands of children. Their actions have consequences beyond the experience of many domestic evaluators. All the more reason to do it right.

References

Alkin, M. C. "National Quality Indicators: A World View." *Studies in Educational Evaluation,* 1988, *14* (1), 11–24.

Chambers, R. "Rapid Rural Appraisal: Rationale and Repertoire." *Public Administration and Development,* 1981, *1,* 95–106.

Chapman, D. W. "Education Data Quality in the Third World: A Five-Country Study." Paper presented at the annual meeting of the American Educational Research Association, San Francisco, Mar. 1989.

Chapman, D. W., and Boothroyd, R. A. "Threats to Data Quality in Developing Country Settings." *Comparative Education Review,* 1988a, 32 (4), 416–429.

Chapman, D. W., and Boothroyd, R. A. "Evaluation Dilemmas: Conducting Evaluation Studies in Developing Countries." *Evaluation and Program Planning,* 1988b, *11,* 37–42.

Chapman, D. W., and Dhungana, M. "The Quality and Use of Education Data in Nepal." Unpublished manuscript, School of Education, State University of New York, Albany, 1989.

Chapman, D. W., Gaal, A. H., Burchfield, S., and Messec, J. "Education Data Quality in Somalia." Unpublished manuscript, School of Education, State University of New York, Albany, 1989.

Government of Botswana. *Botswana Education and Human Resources Sector Assessment.* Tallahassee: Improving the Efficiency of Education Systems Project, Florida State University, 1984.

Government of Liberia. *Liberia Education and Human Resources Sector Assessment.* Tallahassee: Improving the Efficiency of Education Systems Project, Florida State University, 1988.

Habte, A., and Fuller, B. *Educational Policy Change: Raising School Quality and Efficiency.* Washington, D.C.: World Bank, in press.

Imboden, N. *Managing Information for Rural Development Projects.* Paris: Organization for Economic Co-Operation and Development, 1980.

Improving the Efficiency of Education Systems Project. *Final Report of the Improving the Efficiency of Education Systems Project.* Submitted to the Office of Education, Bureau of Science and Technology, U.S. Agency for International Development. Washington, D.C.: Government Printing Office, 1989.

Pigozzi, M. J., and Cieutat, V. J. *Education and Human Resource Sector Assessment Manual.* Tallahassee: Improving the Efficiency of Education Systems Project, Florida State University, 1988.

Windham, D. W. *Indicators of Educational Effectiveness and Efficiency.* Tallahassee: Improving the Efficiency of Education Systems Project, Florida State University, 1988.

DAVID W. CHAPMAN *is associate professor of education at the State University of New York, Albany, where he teaches program evaluation in the Department of Educational Theory and Practice. He has worked in technical assistance activities in over sixteen developing countries.*

Analysis of the nature and variations of investigative characteristics can shed new light on the improvement of evaluation theory and practice.

Analysis of Investigative Features of Select Evaluation Studies

Deborah M. Fournier

This chapter examines the nature and variations of investigative inquiry as evidenced in the examples of Chapters Two through Six in this volume. The aim is to examine how this investigative theme sheds new light on the continuing improvement of evaluation theory and practice. There are several levels at which to approach this analysis; for example, each investigative aspect mentioned by Smith (Chapter One) could easily be treated in a chapter by itself. However, due to space constraints, this chapter focuses primarily on the *process* aspect of inquiry, the nature of the *phenomena,* and the *reasoning.* These emphases touch on and pull in some of the other characteristics mentioned by Smith, such as context, purpose, and the various investigative means (knowledge, observation, reasoning, and intuition), but they also single out what is particularly illuminating and worthy of future examination.

The Investigative Process

Each of the five previous chapters in this volume initiates the inquiry with a problem to be solved, for instance, determining if the program director misused company travel protocols as alleged, discovering the impact of a rural reading project, pinpointing the extent and source of fraudulent practices that may exist within the Medicare system, circumscribing the nature and scope of homelessness, and exposing factors that will facilitate or constrain the attainment of a country's program objectives.[1] Although initiated by a general problem, the process raises a plethora of multifaceted problems as the inquiry proceeds.

NEW DIRECTIONS FOR PROGRAM EVALUATION, no. 56, Winter 1992 © Jossey-Bass Publishers

What process is used to address these problems? Fetterman (Chapter Two), who provides much insight into the "how" of his inquiry, clearly uses archival material, key informant interviews, and so on in linking and weaving information about past behavior in all four of his examples. In the case of the travel fraud, the program director's past activities were reconstructed from numerous document sources such as reimbursement records, travel documents, canceled checks, and petty cash receipts. In tracking via document analysis, Fetterman was led from the director to the hired consultant, to the missing home address, and finally to the county assessor's office. What is noteworthy is that this characteristic tracking and weaving is not linear, as the term might imply, but rather fluid, cyclical, and circuitous. Thus, there is the revisiting and reinterpretation of old evidence, the staging of interviews, and the surprise of new questions not previously entertained.[2] Notice how this weaving process depends on the assumption that an individual's behavior leaves telltale signs that can be traced at a later point in time.

In collecting evidence, each track or step oriented Fetterman to the next step, so he knew how to proceed based on what he found. Schwandt (Chapter Three) also suggests a similar pattern in that "decisions about data collection (whom to interview, what to observe, what documents to examine) were made on a daily basis as the result of the previous day's investigation" (p. 31). And Rog (Chapter Five), at a more general level, describes a spiraling effect where "each activity should provide direction for the next set of activities" (p. 59) and where the process aims "to formulate and reformulate a conceptualization of the program as the activities evolve" (p. 60).

Each step is a result of what was learned from the step preceding it, and each step in turn establishes a context that orients the next step ("doubly contextual"). In terms of how and where to proceed only one step at a time, the investigative process is emergent rather than preordinate. Smith (Chapter One) calls this the "recursively sequential" aspect of investigative inquiry and highlights the second assumption that behavior is primarily purposeful, not random.

Unique or unusual findings also can forcefully reorient the direction of an investigation. For instance, when Fetterman was examining the director's budget and reimbursement records, he found it unusual that the consultant's checks were not sent to his home or business address, that the director had not resided at the recorded place for some time, and that there was odd partial handwriting on the director's travel itinerary. These unexpected, unique findings constituted a red flag to immediately direct resources toward a closer examination of related evidence.

In tracking via key informants in the case of the methodological differences with a sponsor, Fetterman worked with the key informants in order to piece together a history of nonpayment for services rendered.

Likewise, Schwandt suggests that he was responsive to "cues to particular aspects of the division's goals and procedures in need of attention, and as points of departure for the search for patterns" (p. 35). Two additional assumptions are evident here, namely, that individuals are part of a larger social network and that their connection to others is not unintentional but instead purposeful. In other words, there is an assumption of purposeful interaction and an assumption of the constancy of behavior.

Chapters Two through Six suggest a problem-initiated, emergent (one does not know what one is going to do next until the current step is completed), and iterative or recursively sequential (weaving, cyclical, spiraling) process. In turn, this inquiry process entails assumptions that can be characterized as follows: Action or behavior leave tracks that can be traced at some later point in time. Each step orients the inquiry to the next step. People act for a reason (with intent) most of the time (purposive behavior). An individual's social connection to others is for a purpose (purposive interaction). And there is constancy of behavior or the nature of things.

The Nature of the Phenomena

Where Fetterman and Schwandt provide insights into the how of the process, Rog (Chapter Five) and Chapman (Chapter Six) share more in terms of when and where the investigative approach is most useful and beneficial. Both of these chapters allow us to explore the nature of social and educational programming and the difficulties that might impede the investigative process. The discussions highlight difficulties in conducting evaluations, such as the complex and evolving nature of the phenomena under study; the problem of information and evidence that are insufficient, inadequate, or nonexistent for solving the problem at hand; and the difficulty of assembling everything known into a persuasive and useful argument that can guide decisions. Examination of the nature of the phenomena under investigation in evaluation frequently illuminates, albeit indirectly, further process characteristics of the investigative theme in evaluation.

In Rog's study, little is known about the scope, nature, and magnitude of the homeless and mentally ill. An understanding of their characteristics is a crucial first step in the development of appropriate program delivery systems and policy initiatives needed to ameliorate these social problems. Thus, the goal of the investigative inquiry is to gain knowledge about an unknown or hidden population, a goal pursued within the role of an applied social science that aims to guide program and policy development.

Working from a weak knowledge base where little is known a priori about an unknown population, Rog proceeds by "arraying activities in a number of directions and involving multiple and various methods of inquiry" (p. 58) to gain an understanding of the social phenomenon of homelessness, which she characterizes as complex, ever changing, marked by high uncertainty, and unamenable to investigator control. As these multiple lines of inquiry are explored, "information developed from subsequent efforts becomes more refined, of higher quality, and more specific . . . [and] may become less emergent and more confirmatory in nature" (p. 59). So there is the interchange between exploratory and confirmatory phases as the divergent inquiry process slowly gives way to a convergence on the strongest or best supported explanation.[3]

Similarly with Chapman, the nature of the phenomena confronted is complex, multi-problem-oriented, nonstationary, and inaccessible in terms of needed information.[4] As with Rog, the investigative goal is still the same, that is, to uncover relationships, events, and patterns that are hidden due to a lack of knowledge or to the intentional obscuring of information by managers interviewed during the course of the inquiry. The role of the investigation again involves applied social science that identifies contingencies that will shape, facilitate, or constrain movement toward program intervention initiatives, but now in an international setting. The inquiry strives to determine which type of intervention best addresses the multiple needs of the sector. So the purpose (goals and roles) and characterization of the phenomena are in Chapman's case similar to those expressed by Rog.

Both Rog's and Chapman's inquiries examine nonstationary phenomena, that is, complex situations that are changing and evolving as the investigations proceed. In one sense, they are looking forward and making inferences and judgments based on limited data. This highly inferential reasoning is another characteristic of investigative inquiry.

The cases presented by Fetterman, Mangano (Chapter Four), and Schwandt provide a different sense of the phenomena under investigation. In Fetterman's cases, the goal is to make known what is hidden due to deception.[5] The role of the inquiry is to "untangle a web of misdirection and intrigue and to weave a strong fabric of evidence" (p. 16); that is, to gather evidence that can be used for prosecution in a court of law. The inquiry proceeds to examine events bound in time: "Did so-and-so do such-and-such as alleged?" In other words, the phenomena do not change—they are stationary—and the inquiry strives to establish that the events did occur. The inquiry begins with an accusation that is investigated through a reconstructing of past events. It is a retrospective analysis of past events where circumscribed parameters designate the field of inquiry. This distinction is analogous to the differences between conducting survey research and conceptual research. In survey research, the design sets and structures the boundaries, whereas in conceptual research, these limits are fuzzy, unclear, and less directive.

For Mangano, both criminal investigators and evaluators examine behavior retrospectively in the various procedural processes of the durable medical supplier (for example, the provider number process). For the criminal investigator, the problem is, "Did so-and-so do such-and-such as alleged?" For the evaluator, the problem is, "In what ways have the proper procedures been or not been followed?" As in Fetterman's cases, these are events bound in time—stationary phenomena that are different from the nonstationary situations encountered by Rog and Chapman.

Similarly, Schwandt looks to the past in order to examine the impact of a program. However, this case is different from the cases of Fetterman and Mangano in that this is less of an event and more like a situation. A situation entails a variety of events and their interrelationships. Schwandt characterizes the training program in the Eastern Technology example as "moving during most of my stay on-site. The organizations' wants and needs were evolving as the entire organization underwent an identity crisis" (p. 32). Here the phenomenon is nonstationary, but the inquiry seems to use more of a time-bound retrospective approach.

In analyzing each of the cases presented in Chapters Two through Six, we recognize that the nature of the phenomena varies, which presents different kinds of problems in drawing inferences and in justifying evaluation conclusions. Each of these authors can be seen to pose a different inferential problem in a different context concerning different phenomena. This analysis of the nature of investigative phenomena illustrates the important issue of time and the influence of *temporality* on investigations in evaluation.

The examples illustrate that an investigative inquiry in evaluation may encompass a stationary approach to an event bounded in time (Fetterman and Mangano), a stationary approach to a complex, changing situation (Schwandt), or a nonstationary approach to a complex, changing situation (Rog and Chapman). Closer inspection of the implications and trade-offs of each of these scenarios is an intriguing future step in our understanding of the investigative theme in evaluation.

Reasoning

Due in part to the complexity of phenomena and the emergent nature of evidence as discussed briefly above, investigative reasoning seems highly inferential and housed within the realm of informal logic.[6] In this section, I begin at a general level to examine possible modes of investigative reasoning as evidenced in the prior five chapters. I then focus on two noteworthy issues raised by the authors: motives and the use of rapid appraisal and response.

In examining modes of investigative reasoning, we can look again to Fetterman, since he provides a step-by-step account of the inquiry process. Consider the second case that he presents—the program director misusing travel funds. First, Fetterman seems to generate "levels of hypotheses" (primary and secondary—or intermediate) as new evidence is brought to bear on the inquiry. The major hypothesis is that the director is possibly misusing travel funds. During his investigation, another unexpected hypothesis arises, namely, the possibility of a personal association between the director and consultant (that is, a conflict of interest), and he pursues this hypothesis to determine if it is true (this situation seems to imply a hunch). In the case of the faculty physician, the inquiry begins with assertions that there might be violations of the university's consulting policy. Again, during the investigation, another hypothesis arises, which is the possibility of the falsification of medical records for monetary gain, leading Fetterman to pursue this new line of thought. (Note that inferential problems are usually hierarchical in nature.)

It is somewhat unclear as to how all these new hypotheses are generated and pursued; however, Fetterman clearly points out that throughout the inquiry process "the single most important ingredient was instinct. I followed my instincts to analyze, judge, and respond to the physician's behavior and his style of playing the game. Guesses and hunches were invaluable as I followed one lead after the next" (p. 25). He allows himself to trust in, and repeatedly follow, hunches. "Once again, however, instinct provided a useful tool (along with informants and common sense) in identifying and collecting appropriate and useful evidence" (p. 25).

The source of fruitful hunches and guesses may be partly revealed by Fetterman's reliance on what he calls common sense. For example, in the case of the program director, "Common sense and a normative standard suggested that it was highly unlikely that the director would book a first-class seat for the consultant . . . while she traveled in coach on the same flight" (p. 20).

In another instance, common sense is used to put himself "in the physician's shoes and think the way that he thought. I was better able to predict his responses and then to successfully apply that same internal logic to his past indiscretions. Instinct provided a clue and a logic for his behavior" (p. 25). Common sense suggests and seems to orient Fetterman about what might be relevant to explore more closely (the hunch), as well as where to look for evidence. So we might say that his hunches are well-informed guesses, not matters of happenstance. Likewise, in the case of the uncooperative program sponsor, it is after inconstant, untenable demands and erratic behavior that "it became clear that something else was going on besides a methodological difference of opinion and a power play" (p. 17). It is at this point that his investigation is prompted by a hunch.[7]

During the investigation, information arose that could not be explained by the current line of reasoning (information inconsistent with prior information), such as the discovery that the director and "the consultant typically had adjoining rooms on all of their trips" (p. 20), which led Fetterman to the idea that there might possibly be a conflict of interest here. So he begins to entertain the possibility that the director and consultant have some sort of association. He sets out to find evidence that might support that new hypothesis.

This creative process of acting on hunches and guesses or generating a new hypotheses in an attempt to account for new, unexplainable, or unusual evidence seems similar to what Peirce terms *abductive* reasoning (Sebeok and Umiker-Sebeok, 1983). Peirce coined this term as a type of reasoning distinct from induction or deduction because neither of these two patterns of reasoning could account for creative or imaginative thought processes continually used throughout the inquiry process. Peirce contended that abductive reasoning is the process by which new ideas are generated and serves to warrant "entertaining the question interrogatively." But how did he decide if the well-informed hunch is actually relevant or useful?

It seems that what follows from this inventive phase is the use of the newly generated hypothesis as the basis for deducing new kinds of evidence, thus a *deductive* mode of reasoning. In other words, the hypothesis allows one to deduce new kinds of evidence or the expected consequences of such a hypothesis by setting expectations of what one should find if the new hypothesis is in fact true. For example, consider Fetterman's third case study, where the physician's wife is alleged to be on the payroll even though she does not work at the university. He deduces using common sense that if this woman were really working, then he should find retrospective reports about her work, office correspondence, and so on. The working hypothesis suggests what kind of evidence to look for. So we might say that investigative inquiry seemingly involves abductive reasoning that generates new hypotheses in light of some information, whereas deductive reasoning generates new evidence in light of that hypothesis (thus confirming informed guesses). Investigative reasoning fluidly moves back and forth between these two reasoning matters as it progressively increases the level of certainty as a defensible case is built. The inquiry seems to begin with hearsay evidence (suggestive level of probability), and by tracing additional confirmatory (and contradictory) evidence, Fetterman builds a pattern of evidence that becomes more probable.

During the Fetterman investigations, hypotheses are generated as evidence comes in (abductive reasoning), and evidence is collected, evaluated, and interpreted to confirm or test the tentative hypothesis (deductive reasoning).[8,9] This evidence is then given to the attorneys to piece together into a case that will stand up in a court of law (inductive reasoning). So it seems that we can speak of three types of reasoning in the investigative inquiry process: abductive, deductive, and inductive. We might say that investigative inference, characterized as exploratory, creative, and discovery-oriented, can be further characterized by a flowing back and forth between abduction and deduction (that is, an inquiry process of discovery and justification in terms of worthy to look at), which is then put to the test using inductive reasoning (that is, an inquiry process of justification within the realm of jurisprudence). This characterization of investigative inference is depicted in Figure 7.1.

Moving from a general look at reasoning, we can now focus on the two issues of motives and the use of rapid appraisal and response. Much of what Fetterman, Mangano, and Chapman express is based on inferences about the motives (intentionality) of behavior. For example, Chapman emphasizes human motivation: "While a content knowledge in the sector is helpful, it is not at all sufficient. The ability to analyze complex relationships, to discern patterns, and to understand cross-impacts among activities are essential skills" (p. 73). He has us recognize the difficulty in trying to attain "a full grasp of these dynamics or . . . the subtler aspects of the linkages that hold certain patterns of behavior in place while allowing others to be easily altered" (p. 68). In similarly dealing with motives, Fetterman, in the case of the sponsor, reconstructs a pattern of past behavior and infers that the "sponsor was thus using the proposal process to secure free evaluation services and apparently had no intention of funding any of these studies" (p. 18). This inference seems much like establishing an individual's modus operandi.

Figure 7.1. Investigative Inference Characterized
by a Flowing Back and Forth Between
Abductive and Deductive Reasoning

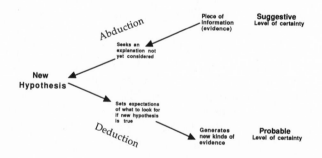

When Chapman is challenged to discern subtleties and nuances within relationships across multiple frameworks (that is, motive, intent, and power) or when Fetterman reconstructs past events, the importance of the role of intuition is underscored.[10] The same might be said about the inquiries pursued by Mangano and Rog. The role of motives and intuition play into the highly inferential reasoning that characterizes investigatory inquiry.

Another aspect of reasoning that is brought out by Mangano, Chapman, and Rog is the notion of rapid appraisal and response. As Chapman observes, "The evaluator must make quick decisions about what things are worth knowing, what things can be ignored, and the level of specificity necessary for those things worth knowing. . . . A balance must be sought between the cost of collecting and ensuring the accuracy of data versus the potential cost of basing decisions on inaccurate data" (p. 71). Here, Chapman focuses on the importance of distinguishing which type of and level of data are needed.

In a similar fashion, Rog points out the necessity of analyzing information as it is collected in order to be able to "respond rapidly to put these courses of action into place" (p. 60). Thus, we get a sense of the necessary expediency of the reasoning employed, which again contributes to the highly inferential characterization of investigative inquiry.

Implications

As stated at the outset of this chapter, there are a number of ways to analyze the examples of investigative inquiry presented in this volume, and likewise there are various ways to address their implications. An investigative theme in evaluation raises intriguing issues such as translation of the notions of flexibility and adaptability in study designs, further clarification of the nature of social and educational programming, warrantability of claims, incorporation of motives, desirability and suitability in varying fields, and space for a "serendipity factor" within evaluation research and practice. There is much more to be learned from the study of similar examples. However, if asked to describe in two words what is most interesting in Chapters Two through Six, we might say *time* and *immersion*. I begin the discussion with the puzzling theme of time, which seemingly underlies the investigative approach to evaluation, and conclude with the second theme of immersion in the phenomena.

Time: "Isn't it about time we get clearer about time?" In this chapter, we have explored phenomena that can be characterized as changing, complex, evolving, hidden, and unknown. We also have discussed the investigative process that the authors of this volume have described as iterative, spiraling, circuitous, incremental, alternatively exploratory and confirmatory, and discovery-oriented—a process that seems conducive to dealing with social and educational programming. Overall, the point is that, in a timely fashion for program, policy, or legal initiatives, evaluators may engage in an evolving process of discovery and exploration regarding complex and emergent phenomena. This influence of temporality in evaluation seems worthy of closer examination.

In Chapter One, Smith points out that evaluation methodology has become increasingly investigative over the past two decades, and he adds that investigative approaches might be more beneficial for complex and dynamic programs than are preordinate, highly controlled approaches. But what is it about these emergent designs that makes them beneficial? Yes, the approach provides flexibility and adaptability, but this description does not seem informative enough. What is it about the investigative approach that makes it attractive to evaluators? The answer, it seems, is that our evaluation task is contingent on time and nonstationary phenomena, thus requiring the flexibility and adaptability of an investigative approach.

In recognizing the nonstationary nature of phenomena, we have alternatives in how to deal with this flux. It has been common to treat nonstationary phenomena as stationary or static. This practice may facilitate communication, and, for the pragmatists' view so prevalent in evaluation, it may work reasonably well as a basis for decisions in some areas. Another alternative commonly employed has been to avoid generalizations or long-range claims and to confine results to a particular local context. Still another alternative is to try to account for the nonstationary nature of the phenomena by approaching them in a nonstationary way.[11] This alternative is the direction in which investigative inquiry seems to be pointing.

Investigative inquiry offers evaluation a closer match between the methodology and the object under study—a nonstationary view of nonstationary phenomena. The terms flexibility and adaptability refer to the ability to freely make changes in the relevance, weight, and meaning of evidence, and in assumptions and inquiry direction. The order in which evidence is collected may not resemble the actual order in which things occurred, and investigative inquiry offers the "floating" designs necessary to order and reconstruct events and relationships. Time impacts on the evidence, assumptions, and arguments that we construct, and investigative inquiry permits time to impact on the process so that we can produce an account that best reflects a reality in flux. (Notice what this suggests about our conception of evaluation as one perspective among the multiple perspectives that make up reality.)

Consider a simple analogy. If we set out to catch fish with a pail or tennis racket, we might catch some fish, such as those in lower water levels or those that we can see from the shoreline. However, we would catch fish much more easily and probably more consistently with a fishing pole and lures since, in the design of these items, the behavior of fish has been taken into account, more so than with other types of tools. It might be that investigative inquiry has recognized the benefits of a pole, and now we are beginning to struggle with refinements, moving from our current wooden stick and simple string line to a better fiberglass pole with casting reel. It is reasonable to say that the kind of phenomena analyzed in evaluations has not changed much over the decades (for example, social and educational programs were just as complex years ago). What has slowly changed is an increase in our understanding and sophistication concerning the phenomena, much like a young child who moves from catching minnows at the shoreline with a pail to catching small fish with a wooden stick and cotton string, graduating to better poles and lures and realizing that there is more to fishing than just catching minnows and small fish off the pier. The point is that in one sense investigative inquiry is a temporal process that gets us to better understand—to really "know"—the phenomena in a personal sense (see Smith's explanation of personal knowledge and context in Chapter One).

Immersion: "Getting to know the chameleon." As discussed earlier, the phenomena studied in evaluation seem changing and emergent on multiple levels and in multiple directions. The use of multiple methods has been suggested to overcome limitations in understanding such chameleonlike objects of study.

The authors in this volume express the importance of immersing oneself in the setting (Fetterman, Schwandt, and Chapman) so as to be able to recognize and accurately interpret evidence. This notion of immersion is also present in the characterizations of the process as weaving, tracking, spiraling, circuitous, and alternatively exploratory and confirmatory. In essence, these investigators are deepening their understanding of the phenomena. They are developing personal knowledge (internalized) where they are "becoming one with" the phenomena.

To clarify this point, consider an example. Someone has acreage to survey in order to construct a topographical map. One way to approach this task is to set up a transit at various points on the land and take the necessary readings over a period of several weekends. Here, the surveyor would be hiking about the land, arriving at key points from which to take readings and in this way seeing the outlay of the land. We might say that it is through the pursuit of the measurement via numerous hikes that the surveyor eventually knows the land.

A different approach is to instead hike all around the land, not just to key points. While hiking, the surveyor might stop and take transit readings from time to time. However, in this approach, he or she is getting a deeper sense of the lay of the land, developing a real "feel" for more than just the topography. Here, the activities may appear the same as in the preceding approach, but the focus is different. We might say that it is through the pursuit of the phenomena via numerous hikes that the surveyor eventually knows the land. This latter approach is what investigative inquiry seems to be like.

The focus of investigative inquiry seems to be the development of an understanding of chameleonlike phenomena. Investigative inquiry can be characterized as a process of progressively becoming acquainted with or immersed in a phenomenon, through which the solution to the study problem emerges as a secondary result. As documented in this volume, the investigative theme in evaluation raises innumerable intriguing issues, all of which will continue to be illuminating and worthy of deeper examination in future dialogues.

Notes

1. Note that the term *problem solving* presupposes the notion of a solution, which may be a bit misleading. In Fetterman's (Chapter Two) case, there is, in a sense, a solution since a contingency question is posed: "Yes or no, is the allegation in fact true?" In contrast, the kinds of questions posed by the other four authors involve a variety of possible, tentative solutions that may change over time in light of new evidence or due to the contextual meaningfulness of the conclusions.

2. Note how in each of Fetterman's cases, unforeseen situations and additional problems unexpectedly arose, which he characterizes as areas of ethical concern, as with the additional discovery of medical fraud in the case of the physician or the falsification of travel documents for personal gain in the case of the program director.

3. Notice the different modes in which arguments are generated and constructed by Fetterman and Mangano as compared with Rog and Chapman. With Fetterman, one gets the sense that knowledge is a process of accretion, assembled as small pieces as in fitting and linking pieces of a puzzle. In contrast, Rog and Chapman do not use the puzzle metaphor; rather, knowledge is more holistic and grows in a complex and comparatively unpredictable and nonlinear way.

Further, it might be that in the four cases that Fetterman presents the problems are more tightly defined and the phenomena are more stable, when compared to the phenomena with which Chapman and Rog deal, which seem more fluid, changing, and multifaceted. In addition, there is a sense in which Fetterman knows the rules of the game before he begins so he is able to be clear about what the parts and the structure of the argument should be and is therefore able to assemble his argument piece by piece. The recursively sequential processes evidenced in Rog's and Chapman's cases seem to involve more amorphously defined phenomena in which the inquiries strive to make sense of complexity and to detect new dimensions. Rog and Chapman appear to be sorting out ideas and developing a broad understanding rather than trying to achieve a simple explanation, as in Fetterman's situation where he is building a case for prosecution to confirm or disconfirm allegations.

4. The nature of the evidence on which conclusions are finally made can vary in degree of reliability and credibility (for example, reasons for distorting facts and investigators' interpretations of what is said in interviews), precision (for example, lack of access to all that might be possible to attain and fuzziness of values, motives, behavior, and preferences), conclusiveness (for example, hearsay or evidence that does not favor one hypothesis over another), reactivity to social factors, and uniqueness or peculiarity, thus fostering a process that is inherently iterative.

5. In each of the five chapters, although the roles may vary, the goals of the inquiries are the same: to make known what is hidden. What differ are the reasons for this concealment. For Fetterman and Mangano, the concealment is due in part to deception. Notice how suspicion

seems to be a motivating factor in the process (more so in Fetterman's portrayal). With Rog, what is hidden is due to a lack of knowledge. This is also true for Chapman, although there is also the sense that some managers may intentionally withhold information for sociopolitical reasons. The investigative role influences the goal (for example, if the role is legal prosecution, what is hidden is perceived as suspicious), and, further, the role (or the game) influences the methods employed (for example, methods in a forensic investigative role might focus on microscopic and chemical analyses, whereas an applied social science role might emphasize the use of interviews or questionnaires).

6. Informal logic (IL) is the analysis of arguments as they occur in everyday language without appeal to more classical, formal conventions of reasoning such as deduction and entailment. Scriven (1986) characterizes probative logic (a new IL) as an attempt to develop a logic of evaluative reasoning.

7. Note the implication of unique or unusual information that signaled him to investigate further. Unique or unusual information may be thought of as an outlier. However, rather than a messy aberration in one's data set, it seems that unique information in investigative inquiry is very much an orienting force in the process, opening up new lines of inquiry not yet considered.

8. Primary hypotheses are not generated, as they are the allegations with which Fetterman begins. At issue here are the additional hypotheses that arise during the investigation into the primary hypothesis (allegation).

9. Fetterman's description of hunches and guesses, as implicitly and explicitly found in his chapter, seems to indicate a merging of reasoning and intuition. In thinking about the complexity and lack of direct accessibility to the phenomena under study, as well as the expertise needed to investigate the phenomena, he seems to place a premium on intuition, as well as highly inferential thinking. However, the role of intuition is not easily discerned in Fetterman's chapter or in any of the other chapters in this volume. This might be due in part to the writing conventions of research ingrained in all of us.

10. Since the evaluations in this volume reflect varying degrees of the investigative aspects highlighted by Smith in Chapter One, I at times make inferential leaps in my analysis (that is, fill in the gaps), as is characterized in this investigative theme. Thus, the identified investigative aspects are, in a way, both the object and the means of the analysis.

11. This notion of the influence of temporality on inquiry seems to add a new dimension to the standard of timeliness of the Joint Committee on Standards for Educational Evaluation (1981). This standard involves releasing evaluation reports when the information is most useful. An additional new dimension might expand this standard to include a different sense of timeliness: timely inferential thinking or being timely in our inquiry. The report may be on time, but the inferences and conclusions drawn may not be (that is, they may not account for the temporality within inquiry). If one is working with dynamic programs, then it seems an important feature of the evaluation should be judgments that take temporality into consideration.

References

Joint Committee on Standards for Educational Evaluation. *Standards for Evaluations of Educational Programs, Projects, and Materials.* New York: McGraw-Hill, 1981.

Scriven, M. S. "Probative Logic." In F. H. van Eemeren, R. Grootendorst, J. A. Blair, and C. A. Williard (eds.), *Argumentation: Across the Lines of Discipline.* Dordrecht, The Netherlands: Foris, 1986.

Sebeok, T. A., and Umiker-Sebeok, J. " 'You Know My Method': A Juxtaposition of Charles S. Peirce and Sherlock Holmes." In U. Eco and T. A. Sebeok (eds.), *The Sign of Three: Dupin, Holmes, Peirce.* Bloomington: Indiana University Press, 1983.

DEBORAH M. FOURNIER is a graduate fellow at Syracuse University and past editorial assistant of New Directions for Program Evaluation.

INDEX

Ordering Information

New Directions for Program Evaluation is a series of paperback books that presents the latest techniques and procedures for conducting useful evaluation studies of all types of programs. Books in the series are published quarterly in spring, summer, fall, and winter and are available for purchase by subscription as well as by single copy.

Subscriptions for 1992 cost $48.00 for individuals (a savings of 20 percent over single-copy prices) and $70.00 for institutions, agencies, and libraries. Please do not send institutional checks for personal subscriptions. Standing orders are accepted.

Single copies cost $17.95 when payment accompanies order. (California, New Jersey, New York, and Washington, D.C., residents please include appropriate sales tax.) Billed orders will be charged postage and handling.

Discounts for quantity orders are available. Please write to the address below for information.

All orders must include either the name of an individual or an official purchase order number. Please submit your order as follows:
    Subscriptions: specify series and year subscription is to begin
    Single copies: include individual title code (such as PE1)

Mail all orders to:
    Jossey-Bass Publishers
    350 Sansome Street
    San Francisco, California 94104

For sales outside of the United States contact:
    Maxwell Macmillan International Publishing Group
    866 Third Avenue
    New York, New York 10022

OTHER TITLES AVAILABLE IN THE
NEW DIRECTIONS FOR PROGRAM EVALUATION SERIES
Nick L. Smith, *Editor-in-Chief*